944.04   6865

Dawson, Philip, comp.
   The French Revolution. Englewood Cliffs, N.J.,
Prentice-Hall [1967]
   vii,181p.   21cm.   (Sources of civilization
in the West)

   A Spectrum book.
   Bibliography:p.180-181.

   1.France-Hist.-Revolution, 1789-1799-Sources.
I.Title.
944.04 D27f
   DC141.D3   67-18698

SOURCES OF CIVILIZATION IN THE WEST

Crane Brinton and Robert Lee Wolff,
General Editors

PHILIP DAWSON, the editor of this volume,
received his A.B. from the University of Michigan
and his Ph.D. from Harvard University. He is
Assistant Professor of History at Stanford University and a contributor to scholarly discussion of
the French Revolution in historical journals.

ALREADY PUBLISHED

FORTHCOMING VOLUMES

THE
FRENCH
REVOLUTION

Edited by

Philip Dawson

PRENTICE-HALL, INC.
Englewood Cliffs, New Jersey

A SPECTRUM BOOK

FOREWORD

The French Revolution and the slightly earlier American Revolution are still in a sense contemporary. The "principles of 1776 and 1789" are still alive and have still, as in the eighteenth century, to struggle against opposing forces. But "principles," or that depreciatory word the scornful would substitute for it—"ideologies"—are not abstract, unreal "forces." They are real because they are embodied in the consciousness—and perhaps through conditioning, in the unconscious—of living human beings. It is the great service of Professor Dawson's well-chosen set of contemporary documents of the French Revolution to bring before the reader the live human beings who made, and who were made in part by, these great events. He leaves to other such source books the "official" documents, the debates, the registers of formal institutional developments, all of course of great importance and readily available. He has instead gone to the "grass roots" more often, since the French Revolution was so urban a movement, the roots that lie metaphorically beneath the pavements, in streets, homes, and public buildings. Here you will find "what really happened" to ordinary human beings, how they fared in the midst of the troubles the Revolution brought to them, as well as the opportunities, hopes, and heroisms those great days brought them. If you will exercise your imagination on the materials here brought before you, you should be better able to understand, better than you could otherwise in the midst of a stable society like our own, what the many revolutions of our own day mean in the lives of those who undergo them.

Crane Brinton
Professor of History
Harvard University

CONTENTS

vii

THE
FRENCH
REVOLUTION

Introduction

The documents in this volume have been chosen for the light they throw upon revolutionary political change in France from 1789 to 1795. It is true that the revolutions of the last quarter of the eighteenth century require a vast perspective, reaching across hundreds of years and thousands of miles. Intelligent consideration of the period still depends, however, on understanding certain events within France that can, in the first place, usefully be analyzed with only slight reference to the larger context. Their particular nature deserves special attention now just as much as it did when, more than a century ago, Tocqueville devoted his concluding pages to the character of the French people, "the most brilliant and the most dangerous of the nations of Europe."

Two kinds of revolutionary change occurred in France. There was repeated violent seizure, contrary to existing law, of effective political power. There were also rapid and extensive changes in institutional structure, in the distribution and rights of property, in attitudes and beliefs; altogether these changes affected more or less profoundly the legal and customary relations within and between social groupings, from family and local community to nation. Many events had a revolutionary character, and the very word "revolution" came to connote a way of life.

The ultimate aim of a revolutionary must be a new order that will be stable. Indeed, the desire to solve once and for all existing public problems was widespread in France in the early 1790's. Fundamental issues rose to the surface of public life. Successive governments grappled with them, but their solutions necessarily consisted in a delicate balance of contrary purposes, a balance that could be maintained only so long as the opposing tensions were roughly equal. In actuality, they did not remain equal, and the recurrent use of force tended to upset whatever balance had been achieved and to initiate new changes in the structure of government and the distribution of political power. The new changes

called forth opponents who were tempted to resort to force, and
the authorities used force against them. Hence there was an oscil-
lating pattern of events—peaceable, or at least lawful, efforts to
reform public life, and violent efforts to gain or keep political
power. The chapters in this book alternate between these two
kinds of revolutionary change. Organizing the material in this
way is intended to facilitate comparison of the successive situations
and outbursts that occurred, and thus make measurable the great
political distance traversed in these seven years.

These themes would scarcely suffice to determine a selection
from, for example, the 25,000 items in print listed by Tourneux
merely for the history of Paris in the revolutionary period. I have
made it a rule to exclude memoirs, because they require elaborate
critical verification, and legislative enactments, because the major
ones are all available in English translations by John Hall Stewart.
This, therefore, is a selection of statements, made during the revolution, intended to report or persuade. Some of them have been chosen
to exemplify evidence that fills many printed pages and is rarely
read in its entirety: for example, grievance lists or police reports.
Others are historic statements in that they are among the principal
sources of information about major political events and are relied
on, directly or indirectly, by all historians of those events.

The central place given to politics here has resulted in a heavy
emphasis on the history of Paris rather than the provincial cities
and on articulate participants more than the many people who
were affected but were powerless. This emphasis is traditional in
older historical writing. It has some other justification, since events
in Paris and deliberate choices by articulate individuals decisively
affected revolutionary politics everywhere else, and the sequence
of these events and choices is a convenient narrative framework.

Little of the material here has previously appeared in English.
Some of the difficulties, which occasionally seem insuperable, of
translating Revolutionary French are described very well by James
Matthew Thompson, *The French Revolution* (Oxford: 1943), pp.
v-vii, and by one of his former students in the *Times Literary
Supplement*, LXVI (1967), 18. The translations in this volume are
mine; where they particularly require explanation, it is placed in
brackets. It was very helpful, in revising my versions of Robespierre's
speech and a few shorter documents in Parts V and VI, to refer

to previous translations by Melvin A. Edelstein, Laurence R. Veysey, Mack Walker, and Mrs. Richard Helmstadter. I am grateful also to J.-B. Baillière et fils, publishers of *Information Historique*, for permission to include a translation of a letter first edited in it.

The value of this selection rests essentially on the investigations and critical judgments of other scholars—French for the most part —who have rescued the whole subject from the narrow confines of contemporary party politics and made it widely comprehensible as human experience.

Part One

🌿 FRANCE ON THE EVE
OF REVOLUTION

The origins of the Revolution of 1789 can be traced back more than seven centuries. By 1787 it was obvious that France was on the verge of great events. Rarely in history has a pre-revolutionary state of affairs given rise to evidence so voluminous and informative as that which is available concerning the years 1787-1789.

The selections here all deal with one local area, around Orléans, and have been chosen to exemplify three important types of evidence: contemporary analysis by an intelligent observer, statistical data drawn from tax records, and complaints reported at the time of the election of the deputies to the Estates-General.

Arthur Young, *Travels in France*

In the extensive and varied literature of travelers and tourists of the eighteenth century, a special place is occupied by the work of Arthur Young, that indefatigable collector of facts, shrewd observer of humanity, and zealous reformer of agriculture. He traveled widely in England and Ireland before having the historic luck to begin his tour of France on the very eve of the most decisive political events there in several centuries. His travel journal, kept concurrently, is followed by twenty topical chapters written later. The brief excerpts here are, except for one paragraph, from the journal. They begin with his first arrival in Paris on May 25, 1787, and the first week of his southward journey, which was to proceed to Spain by way of Limoges and Toulouse. Coming back through Bordeaux and Poitiers, he regained the valley of the

Loire toward the end of the summer and, on September 12, left
Chambord on his way to Paris. He passed quickly through the
metropolis in order to reach Liancourt, where he stayed for three
weeks as a guest of the La Rochefoucauld family. Returning to
Paris again on October 11, 1787, he spent the rest of that month
obtaining a fuller view of the city.

The following selections are from Arthur Young, *Travels during
the Years 1787, 1788, and 1789, Undertaken More Particularly with
a View of Ascertaining the Cultivation, Wealth, Resources, and
National Prosperity of the Kingdom of France,* 2nd ed. (London:
1794), I, 8-12, 68-69, 76-80, 539.

. . . The last ten miles I was eagerly on the watch for
that throng of carriages which near London impede the traveller.
I watched in vain; for the road, quite to the gates, is, on comparison,
a perfect desert. So many great roads join here that I suppose this
must be accidental. The entrance has nothing magnificent; ill built
and dirty. To get to the Rue de Varenne, Faubourg Saint-Germain,
I had the whole city to cross, and passed it by narrow, ugly, and
crowded streets.

At the hôtel de La Rochefoucauld I found the Duke of Liancourt
and his sons, the Count de La Rochefoucauld and the Count Alexander, with my excellent friend Monsieur Lazowski, all of whom I
had the pleasure of knowing in Suffolk. They introduced me to
the Duchess d'Estissac, mother of the Duke of Liancourt, and to
the Duchess of Liancourt. The agreeable reception and friendly
attentions I met with from all this liberal family were well calculated to give me the most favourable impression.

May 26. So short a time had I passed before in France that the
scene is totally new to me. Till we have been accustomed to travel-
ling, we have a propensity to stare at and admire everything—and
to be on the search for novelty, even in circumstances in which it
is ridiculous to look for it. I have been upon the full silly gape to
find out things that I had not found before, as if a street in Paris
could be composed of anything but houses or houses formed of
anything but brick or stone—or that the people in them, not being
English, would be walking on their heads. I shall shake off this
folly as fast as I can and bend my attention to mark the character
and disposition of the nation. Such views naturally lead us to catch
the little circumstances which sometimes express them; not an easy
task, but subject to many errors.

I have only one day to pass at Paris, and that is taken up with buying necessaries. . . .

After a rapid excursion, with my friend Lazowski, to see many things, but too hastily to form any correct idea, spent the evening at his brother's, where I had the pleasure of meeting Monsieur Broussonet, secretary of the Royal Society of Agriculture, and Monsieur Desmarets, both of the Academy of Sciences. As Monsieur Lazowski is well informed in the manufactures of France, in the police of which he enjoys a post of consideration, and as the other gentlemen have paid much attention to agriculture, the conversation was in no slight degree instructive, and I regretted that a very early departure from Paris would not let me promise myself a further enjoyment so congenial with my feelings as the company of men whose conversation showed a marked attention to objects of national importance. On the breaking up of the party, went with Count Alexander de La Rochefoucauld post to Versailles, to be present at the fête of the day following (Whitsunday); slept at the Duke of Liancourt's hôtel.

May 27. Breakfasted with him at his apartments in the palace, which are annexed to his office of grand master of the wardrobe, one of the principal in the court of France. Here I found the duke surrounded by a circle of noblemen, among whom was the Duke de La Rochefoucauld, well known for his attention to natural history; I was introduced to him, as he is going to Bagnères-de-Luchon in the Pyrenees, where I am to have the honour of being in his party.

The ceremony of the day was the King's investing the Duke of Berry, son of the Count d'Artois, with the *cordon bleu* [badge of the Knights of the royal Order of the Holy Spirit]. The Queen's band was in the chapel where the ceremony was performed, but the musical effect was thin and weak. During the service the King was seated between his two brothers and seemed by his carriage and inattention to wish himself a-hunting. He would certainly have been as well employed as in hearing afterwards from his throne a feudal oath of chivalry, I suppose, or some such nonsense, administered to a boy of ten years old. . . .

After this ceremony was finished, the King and the knights walked in a sort of procession to a small apartment in which he dined, saluting the Queen as they passed. There appeared to be more ease and familiarity than form in this part of the ceremony;

Her Majesty, who, by the way, is the most beautiful woman I saw today, received them with a variety of expression. On some she smiled; to others she talked; a few seemed to have the honour of being more in her intimacy. Her return to some was formal, and to others distant. . . . The ceremony of the King's dining in public is more odd than splendid. The Queen sat by him with a cover before her but ate nothing, conversing with the Duke of Orléans and the Duke of Liancourt, who stood behind her chair. To me it would have been a most uncomfortable meal, and were I a sovereign, I would sweep away three-fourths of these stupid forms; if kings do not dine like other people, they lose much of the pleasure of life; their station is very well calculated to deprive them of much, and they submit to nonsensical customs, the sole tendency of which is to lessen the remainder. . . .

The palace of Versailles, one of the objects of which report had given me the greatest expectation, is not in the least striking. I view it without emotion: the impression it makes is nothing. What can compensate the want of unity? From whatever point viewed, it appears an assemblage of buildings; a splendid quarter of a town, but not a fine edifice. . . . The whole palace, except the chapel, seems to be open to all the world; we pushed through an amazing crowd of all sorts of people to see the procession, many of them not very well dressed, whence it appears that no questions are asked. But the officers at the door of the apartment in which the King dined made a distinction and would not permit all to enter promiscuously.

Travellers speak much, even very late ones, of the remarkable interest the French take in all that personally concerns their King, showing by the eagerness of their attention not curiosity only, but love. Where, how, and in whom those gentlemen discovered this I know not. It is either misrepresentation, or the people are changed in a few years more than is credible. Dine at Paris. . . .

May 28. Finding my mare sufficiently recovered for a journey, a point of importance to a traveller so weak in cavalry as myself, I left Paris, accompanying the Count de La Rochefoucauld and my friend Lazowski, and commencing a journey that is to cross the whole kingdom to the Pyrenees. The road to Orléans is one of the greatest that leads from Paris; I expected, therefore, to have my former impression of the little traffic near that city removed; but on the contrary it was confirmed; it is a desert compared with those around London. In ten miles we met not one stage or diligence, only two messageries, and very few chaises; not a tenth of what would have been met had we been leaving London at the same hour. Knowing how great, rich, and important a city Paris is, this circumstance perplexes me much. Should it afterwards be confirmed, conclusions in abundance are to be drawn.

For a few miles, the scene is everywhere scattered with the shafts of quarries, the stone drawn up by lanthorn wheels of a great diameter. The country diversified, and its greatest want to please the eye is a river; woods generally in view; the proportion of the French territory covered by this production for want of coals must be prodigious, for it has been the same all the way from Calais. . . . 20 miles.

May 29. To Étampes is partly through a flat country, the beginning of the famous Pays de Beauce. To Toury, flat and disagreeable, only two or three gentlemen's seats in sight.—31 miles.

May 30. One universal flat, uninclosed, uninteresting, and even tedious, though small towns and villages are everywhere in sight; the features that might compound a landscape are not brought together. This Pays de Beauce contains, by reputation, the cream of French husbandry; the soil excellent; but the management all fallow. Pass through part of the forest of Orléans belonging to the duke of that name; it is one of the largest in France.

From the steeple of the cathedral at Orléans, the prospect is very fine. The town large, and its suburbs, of single streets, extend near a league. The vast range of country that spreads on every side is an unbounded plain, through which the magnificent Loire bends his stately way, in sight for 14 leagues; the whole scattered with rich meadows, vineyards, gardens, and forests. The population must be very great; for, beside the city, which contains near 40,000 people, the number of smaller towns and villages strewed thickly over the plain is such as to render the whole scene animated. The cathedral, from which we had this noble prospect, is a fine building, the choir raised by Henry IV. The new church is a pleasing edifice; the bridge a noble structure of stone, and the first experiment of the flat arch made in France, where it is now so fashionable. . . . There are many barges and boats at the quay, built upon the river in the Bourbonnais, loaded with wood, brandy, wine, and other goods;

on arriving at Nantes, the vessels are broken up and sold with the cargo. Great numbers built with spruce fir. A boat goes from hence to that city when demanded by six passengers, each paying a *louis-d'or* [20 *livres*]; they lie on shore every night and reach Nantes in four days and a half. The principal street leading to the bridge is a fine one, all busy and alive.

[In a later chapter, Arthur Young added two paragraphs about manufacturing at Orléans:]

The manufactures are not inconsiderable: they make stockings of all kinds and print linens; a fabric of woollen caps has been established here since Louis XIV's time, in which two houses are employed; the chief we viewed. It employs at home about 300 working hands and 1200 to 1500 others. The caps are entirely made of Spanish wool; three ounces of yarn make a cap; they are all for exportation, from Marseilles to Turkey and the coast of Africa, being worn under turbans; in dressing they extract the grease with urine, full and finish in the manner of cloth.

The sugar refinery is a considerable business; there are 10 large and 17 smaller houses engaged in it; the first employ each 40 to 45 workmen, the latter 10 to 12; one of the principal, which I viewed, makes 600,000 pounds of sugar, and the rest in proportion. The best sugar is from Martinique, but they mix them together. Rum is never made from molasses, which is sold to the Dutch at 3 shillings the pound; the scum is squeezed, and the refuse is spread thick on meadow to kill moss, which it does very effectually. The price of raw sugar is 30 to 45 *livres* per 100 pounds. The coal they burn is from the vicinity of Moulins, in the Bourbonnais. Trade in general is now brisk here.

Admire the fine acacias scattered about the town.—20 miles.

May 31. On leaving it, enter soon the miserable province of Sologne, which the French writers call the *triste* Sologne. Through all this country they have had severe spring frosts, for the leaves of the walnuts are black and cut off. I should not have expected this unequivocal mark of a bad climate after passing the Loire. To La Ferté Lowendhal, a dead flat of hungry sandy gravel, with much heath. The poor people, who cultivate the soil here, are *métayers,* that is, men who hire the land without ability to stock it; the proprietor is forced to provide cattle and seed, and he and his tenant divide the produce; a miserable system that perpetuates poverty

and excludes instruction. . . . To Nouan-le-Fuzelier, a strange mix-
ture of sand and water. Much inclosed, and the houses and cot-
tages of wood filled between the studs with clay or bricks, and
covered not with slate but tile, with some barns boarded like those
in Suffolk—rows of pollards in some of the hedges; an excellent
road of sand; the general features of a woodland country, all combined to give a strong resemblance to many parts of England; but
the husbandry is so little like that of England that the least attention to it destroyed every notion of similarity.—27 miles.

June 1. The same wretched country continues to La Loge; the
fields are scenes of pitiable management, as the houses are of misery.
Yet all this country highly improveable, if they knew what to do
with it; the property, perhaps, of some of those glittering beings
who figured in the procession the other day at Versailles. Heaven
grant me patience while I see a country thus neglected—and forgive
me the oaths I swear at the absence and ignorance of the possessors.

*   *   *

September 12. In two miles from the park wall [of Chambord] regain the high road on the Loire. In discourse with a *vigneron,* we
were informed that it froze this morning hard enough to damage
the vines; and I may observe that for four or five days past the
weather has been constantly clear, with a bright sun and so cold
a north-east wind as to resemble much our cold clear weather in
England in April; we have all our great coats on the whole day.
Dine at Cléry, and view the monument of that able but bloody
tyrant Louis XI, in white marble; he is represented in a kneeling
posture, praying forgiveness, I suppose, which doubtless was promised him by his priests for his basenesses and his murders. Reach
Orléans.—30 miles.

September 13. Here my companions, wanting to return as soon
as possible to Paris, took the direct road thither; but, having
travelled it before, I preferred that by Pithiviers in the way to
Fontainebleau. One motive for my taking this road was its passing
by Denainvilliers, the seat of the late celebrated Monsieur Duhamel,
where he made those experiments in agriculture which he has re-
cited in many of his works. At Pithiviers I was just by it and walked
thither for the pleasure of viewing grounds I had read of so often,
considering them with a sort of classic reverence. His *homme*

d'affaires, who conducted the farm, being dead, I could not get many particulars to be depended upon. Monsieur Fougeroux, the present possessor, was not at home, or I should doubtless have had all the information I wished. I examined the soil, a principal point in all experiments when conclusions are to be drawn from them; and I took also notes of the common husbandry. . . . In an inclosure behind the house is a plantation of various curious exotic trees, finely grown, also several rows of ash, elm, and poplar along the roads near the chateau, all planted by Monsieur Duhamel. It gave me still greater pleasure to find that Denainvilliers is not an inconsiderable estate. The lands extensive; the chateau respectable; with offices, gardens, etc., that prove it the residence of a man of fortune. . . . Four miles before Malesherbes a fine plantation of a row of trees on each side the road begins, formed by Monsieur de Malesherbes, and is a striking instance of attention to the decorating of an open country. More than two miles of them are mulberries. They join his other noble plantations at Malesherbes, which contain a great variety of the most curious trees that have been introduced in France.—36 miles.

*   *   *

October 12. It grows so late in the season that I shall make no other stay here than what will be necessary for viewing public buildings. This will unite well enough with delivering some letters I brought to a few men of science; and it will leave me the evenings for the theatres, of which there are many in Paris. In throwing on paper a rapid *coup d'oeil* of what I see of a city so well known in England, I shall be apt to delineate my own ideas and feelings, perhaps more than the objects themselves; and be it remembered that I profess to dedicate this careless itinerary to trifles much more than to objects that are of real consequence. From the tower of the cathedral, the view of Paris is complete. It is a vast city, even to the eye that has seen London from St. Paul's; a circular form gives an advantage to Paris; but a much greater is the atmosphere. It is now so clear that one would suppose it the height of summer; the clouds of coal-smoke that envelop London always prevent a distinct view of that capital, but I take it to be one-third at least larger than Paris. The buildings of the parlement-house are disfigured by a gilt and tawdry gate and a French roof. The hôtel des monnaies is a fine building and the façade of the Louvre one of the most elegant in the world, because they have (to the eye) no roofs; in proportion as a roof is seen, a building suffers. . . . At night to the opera, which I thought a good theatre till they told me it was built in six weeks [in 1781]; and then it became good for nothing in my eyes, for I suppose it will be tumbling down in six years. . . .

October 13. Across Paris to the Rue des Blancs-Manteaux, to Monsieur Broussonet, secretary of the Society of Agriculture; he is in Burgundy. . . . There has been much rain today; and it is almost incredible, to a person used to London, how dirty the streets of Paris are and how horribly inconvenient and dangerous walking is without a foot-pavement. We had a large party at dinner, with politicians among them, and some interesting conversation on the present state of France. The feeling of everybody seems to be that the archbishop will not be able to do anything towards exonerating the state from the burden of its present situation; some think that he has not the inclination; others that he has not the courage; others that he has not the ability. By some he is thought to be attentive only to his own interest; and by others, that the finances are too much deranged to be within the power of any system to recover, short of the States-General of the kingdom, and that it is impossible for such an assembly to meet without a revolution in the government ensuing. All seem to think that something extraordinary will happen, and a bankruptcy is an idea not at all uncommon. But who is there that will have the courage to make it?

October 14. To the Benedictine abbey of Saint-Germain (-des-Prés], to see pillars of African marble, etc. It is the richest abbey in France: the abbot has 300,000 *livres* a year. I lose my patience at seeing such revenues thus bestowed; consistent with the spirit of the tenth century but not with that of the eighteenth. What a noble farm would a fourth of this income establish! What turnips, what cabbages, what potatoes, what clover, what sheep, what wool! . . . Pass the Bastille; another pleasant object to make agreeable emotions vibrate in a man's bosom. I search for good farmers and run my head at every turn against monks and state prisons. To the Arsenal, to wait on Monsieur Lavoisier, the celebrated chemist. . . .

By the boulevards to the Place Louis XV, which is not properly a square, but a very noble entrance to a great city. The façades of the two buildings erected are highly finished. The union of the Place Louis XV with the Champs Elysées, the gardens of the Tuileries, and the Seine is open, airy, elegant, and superb, and is the most agreeable and best built part of Paris; here one can be clean and breathe freely. But by far the finest thing I have yet seen at Paris is the *halle aux blés,* or corn market [built in 1763-1767, destroyed by fire in 1802]; it is a vast rotunda; the roof entirely of wood, upon a new principle of carpentry, to describe which would demand plates and long explanations; the galley is 150 yards round, consequently the diameter is as many feet: it is as light as if suspended by the fairies. In the grand area wheat, peas, beans, lentils are stored and sold. In the surrounding divisions, flour on wooden stands. You pass by stair-cases doubly winding within each other to spacious apartments for rye, barley, oats, etc. The whole is so well planned and so admirably executed that I know of no public building that exceeds it either in France or England. . . . It has but one fault, and that is situation; it should have been upon the banks of the river, for the convenience of unloading barges without land carriage. In the evening, to the Comédie Italienne; the edifice fine, and the whole quarter regular and new built. . . . Dine with my friend at the Palais Royal at a coffeehouse; well dressed people; everything clean, good, and well served; but here, as everywhere else, you pay a good price for good things. . . . In the evening to . . . the Comédie Française. . . . This theatre, the principal one at Paris, is a fine building, with a magnificent portico. . . .

October 16. To Monsieur Lavoisier, by appointment. . . . In the evening to Monsieur Lomond, a very ingenious and inventive mechanic, who has made an improvement of the jenny for spinning cotton. . . .

October 17. To Monsieur l'abbé Messier, astronomer royal, and of the Academy of Sciences. View the exhibition, at the Louvre, of the Academy's paintings. For one history piece in our exhibitions at London here are ten; abundantly more than to balance the difference between an annual and biennial exhibition. Daniel today with a party whose conversation was entirely political. Monsieur de Calonne's *Requête au Roi* is come over [from London, where he had gone after being dismissed from the ministry], and all the world are reading and disputing on it. It seems, however, generally agreed that, without exonerating himself from the charge of agiotage, he has thrown no inconsiderable load on the shoulders of the Archbishop of Toulouse, the present premier, who will be puzzled to get rid of the attack. But both these ministers were condemned on all hands in the lump as being absolutely unequal to the difficulties of so arduous a period. One opinion pervaded the whole company: that they are on the eve of some great revolution in the government; that everything points to it: the confusion in the finances great, with a deficit impossible to provide for without the States-General of the kingdom, yet no idea formed of what would be the consequence of their meeting; no minister existing, or to be looked to in or out of power, with such decisive talents as to promise any other remedy than palliative ones; a prince on the throne with excellent dispositions but without the resources of a mind that could govern in such a moment without ministers; a court buried in pleasure and dissipation and adding to the distress, instead of endeavouring to be placed in a more independent situation; a great ferment amongst all ranks of men, who are eager for some change without knowing what to look to or to hope for; and a strong leaven of liberty, increasing every hour since the American revolution altogether form a combination of circumstances that promise ere long to ferment into motion if some master hand, of very superior talents and inflexible courage, be not found at the helm to guide events instead of being driven by them. It is very remarkable that such conversation never occurs but a bankruptcy is a topic; the curious question on which is, would a bankruptcy occasion a civil war and a total overthrow of the government? The answers that I have received to this question appear to be just: such a measure, conducted by a man of abilities, vigour, and firmness, would certainly not occasion either one or the other. But the same measure, attempted by a man of a different character, might possibly do both. All agree that the States of the kingdom cannot assemble without more liberty being the consequence, but I meet with so few men who have any just ideas of freedom that I question much the species of this new liberty that is to rise. They know not how to value the privileges of THE PEOPLE; as to the nobility and the clergy, if a revolution added any thing to their scale, I think it would do more mischief than good.

[Later, Young added a footnote to this page of his journal, as follows:]

In transcribing these papers for the press, I smile at some remarks and circumstances which events have since placed in a singular position; but I alter none of these passages; they explain what were the opinions in France, before the revolution, on topics of importance; and the events which have since taken place render them the more interesting. June, 1790.

Landholding in Four Localities near Orléans: Statistical Tables

Quantitative facts that were not readily available to Arthur Young or any of his contemporaries can be reconstructed by historians. They provide a useful test for descriptions like his, and they can serve to suggest new questions. The following tables concern three villages and a small town in the region around Orléans. They were compiled from the rolls for the "twentieth" taxes, one of the few paid by ecclesiastical institutions, priests, and nobles as well as by commoners. There were two twentieth taxes on land, which had been established at different times but which were, by 1789, collected together as a 10 per cent annual tax on estimated income from landed property. The estimates of incomes in the tax rolls were usually understatements whose inaccuracy was variable; the figures for the amounts of land held are more dependable.

The selection here includes one place from each distinctive area in the region. Erceville is in the Beauce; Lion-en-Sullias is on the eastern edge of the Sologne; Pithiviers-le-Vieil is a town in the Gâtinais, an area of varied agriculture northeast of Orléans; and Saint-Jean-de-la-Ruelle is part of the vignoble in the immediate neighborhood of the city. Differences between these localities are apparent in the tables, but all of them shared three characteristics: a large proportion of the total cultivable land was held by nobles; a small proportion was held by peasants; and there were many peasant proprietors.

Data are from Camille Bloch, "La répartition de la propriété foncière à la veille de la Révolution dans quelques paroisses de la généralité d'Orléans," *Revue d'Histoire Moderne et Contemporaine,* II (1900), 246-267, reprinted in his *Études sur l'histoire économique de la France (1760-1789)* (Paris: 1900), 83-116.

Table 1. Taxpayers, by Size of Property and by Economic Class, in Four Parishes in the Bailliage of Orléans

	Sizes of Properties (in arpents)										No. of Tax-payers
	<1	1-10		11-50		51-100		101-200		>200	
	W	U	W	U	W	U	W	U	W		
Erceville	6	3	43	2	10	0	1	0	0	2	67
Lion-en-Sullias	8	7	32	1	7	2	0	3	1	3	64
Pithiviers-le-Vieil	84	15	157	6	40	2	3	4	1	6	318
Saint-Jean-de-la-Ruelle	16	39	47	4	3	0	0	0	0	0	109

KEY:
  U = bourgeois, nobles, and clergy
  W = peasants, artisans and tradesmen
NOTE: The rolls for the twentieth tax listed some taxpayers without indicating the size of their property. These are omitted in Table 1, and hence in the column at the right each total is smaller than the number of all the taxpayers in the village; the complete totals are in Table 2, column Q.

Table 2. Taxpayers, by Status and Residence, in Four Parishes in the Bailliage of Orléans

(for key see p. 18)

	C	N	B	T	P	F	Q
Erceville	3	2	3	17	39	9[a]	74
Lion-en-Sullias	8	5	8[b]	0	46	1	68
Pithiviers-le-Vieil	7	8	23	68	81	132	319
Saint-Jean-de-la-Ruelle	4	4	35	1	63	4	111

[a] Excludes one domestic servant domiciled in Paris
[b] Includes one bourgeois resident in the parish

Table 3. Taxable Property, by Status and Residence of Taxpayers, in Four Parishes in the Bailliage of Orléans

	C	N	B	P & T	F	V
Erceville	27	1464	28	406	75	2002
Lion-en-Sullias	22	1235	376	338	26	1997
Pithiviers-le-Vieil	178	2067	439	1162	485	4331
Saint-Jean-de-la-Ruelle	18	53	286	176	8	541

Tables 2 and 3. KEY:

C = clergy
N = nobles
B = bourgeois not resident in parish
T = tradesmen and artisans
P = peasants resident in parish
F = *forains* (peasants resident in other parishes)

Q = total number of proprietors paying twentieth taxes
V = total number of *arpents* assessed for twentieth taxes

Complaints and Grievances in the Region of Orléans

The elections to the Estates-General were the subject of a royal regulation issued on January 24, 1789, and applied in most of the kingdom, the most important provinces excepted from it being Brittany, Provence, Dauphiné, Alsace and Lorraine. The regulation began with a preamble which stated that the King expected to obtain, through a sequence of assemblies of the Third Estate, "a sort of communication with all the inhabitants of his kingdom" and a more direct familiarity with their needs and desires; that he wanted to follow the procedural precedents of 1614 as much as possible; that "the respect for old usage and the necessity of adapting it to the present circumstances, without injuring the principles of justice, have rendered the organization of the coming Estates-General and the preliminary arrangements all very difficult and often imperfect"; and that the King exhorted the voters to remember "that men of prudent mind deserve their preference and that . . . it is rare in national and public affairs for the most decent men to be the most clever as well."

In its 51 articles, the regulation ordered the officials and judges of the royal courts of first instance, which were entitled *bailliages* in some provinces and *sénéchaussées* in others, to summon each of the three estates and specified the procedures to be followed by them. Each parish priest and monastic establishment could vote for deputies from the First Estate. Every noble could vote in the Second Estate in each *bailliage* where he held property. Those eligible to vote in the elections for the Third Estate would be all other French subjects who were 25 years of age and were included on the tax roll of their locality. In the countryside and the small towns, each community or parish having a separate tax roll would hold a primary assembly, in order to draw up a list of its complaints and grievances and to choose representatives to take this list to the assembly of the Third Estate of the whole *bailliage*. In 290 larger towns, the electoral process involved two preliminary stages: first each corporation would assemble, draw up a list of complaints and grievances, and choose representatives; then these representatives would constitute an assembly for the town to draw up a list of grievances and to choose representatives; finally, the representatives from the town would join those from the country parishes in the electoral assembly for the Third Estate of the *bailliage*.

There were other complications in the process, but only two points need to be noted in order to appreciate the lists of complaints and grievances presented here. At each election in each estate the voters were to draw up such a list, with the result that thousands of these documents have survived. In the Third Estate, the lists of complaints and grievances in each *bailliage* or *sénéchaussée* underwent a filtering process as the successive electoral assemblies examined incoming grievances and prepared new lists to be passed on to the next assembly.

In the Third Estate of the *bailliage* of Orléans, lists of grievances were drawn up by 165 villages. The four lists here come from the villages for which statistical data on taxpayers and landownership have been given. In the city of Orléans, lists were drawn up by forty-two occupational groups and by three other groups: the officers of the militia, the members of the learned society, and 767 residents not belonging to any corporation. The list prepared by the latter group, too long for inclusion here, became the basis for the list of grievances adopted by the town assembly, and that list in turn was adopted with minor changes by the Third Estate of the whole *bailliage*. The grievance lists presented here are arranged in chronological order of their adoption.

The following selections are from *Cahiers de doléances du bailliage d'Orléans pour les États Généraux de 1789*, Camille Bloch, ed. (Orléans: 1906-1907), I, 3-6, 353-355, 623-625, 673-677; II, 84-86.

List of grievances for the Royal Academy of Sciences, Arts, and Letters of Orléans

The electoral meeting was held on Monday, February 23, in the hall at the botanical garden, with 22 members present. A priest, who was a canon of the cathedral and principal of the local *collège*, and six nobles abstained from the deliberations, reserving their respective votes for the assemblies of the First and Second Estates. The members voting were: Henry de Longuêve, king's advocate in the *bailliage* of Orléans, and Defay, a businessman and a naturalist, member of the academies of Berlin and Haarlem (these two were to be elected on March 25 to the Estates-General, among the six deputies from the Third Estate of the *bailliage* of Orléans); Chaufton, professor of law in the University of Orléans; Leblond, a lawyer; Levassor du Bouchet, Trésorier de France at Orléans, and Turmeau, Trésorier de France at Alençon [administrative officials supervising certain financial matters and the royal domain]; Marcaudier, judge in the tax court for the *élection* [*i.e.*, tax district] of Bourges and a member of the Economic Society of Bern; Soyer, chief engineer for dykes and embankments on the Loire; Gallot, a civil engineer; Latour and Maigreau, physicians; Forel de la Croix, a professor of surgery; Dalet, former chief surgeon of the royal troops and hospitals in Haiti; Couret de Villeneuve, a publisher and manager of the newspaper *Affiches Orléanaises*; Prozet, a pharmacist and executive officer of the botanical garden.

If a happy concord reigned between all the Orders of the State, it would be unnecessary to limit the authorization to be given to the deputies from the *bailliage*. But a benefit so desirable does not yet exist. The Nobility of several provinces is declaring a resistance which gives rise to the fear that the existing abuses cannot be reformed, and the Clergy has not yet expressed itself.

The Academy therefore thinks that it is wise to make the deputies' instructions binding as to the principal objectives without which one can scarcely hope to see the regeneration of the kingdom. It proposes, then, to prescribe to the deputies of the Third Estate:

1. To vote in the Estates-General only as three Orders jointly, with the votes counted by head. The need for this restraint, without which one would see particular interest dominate the general interest, is proved by the very resistance of the great nobles; for what can be the cause of their obstinate determination to maintain voting by Order, if not the desire to see the resulting abuses continue? A few writings, doubtless with a view to restoring peace between the three Orders, have proposed voting by head upon taxation and keeping the vote by Order for all other matters. But this palliative is absolutely illusory; for of what use then would be the equality of representation obtained by the Third? Besides, if voting by head is necessary when it involves the mere sacrifice of part of our property, it must be much more important when it is a

question of the liberty, the honor, and the lives of citizens; the capability that would be given each Order of resisting the others would establish in the national Assembly three interests which, incessantly colliding, would end by reducing it to inaction; animosity, replacing the patriotic spirit that ought to reign, would kindle an internal war; the powerful, always seeking to oppress the weak, would cause the interest of the few to triumph over that of the many. Voting by head, on the contrary, putting an end to the vicious distinction between the Orders, would turn all minds toward the public good, which in a well constituted state will always be that of the greatest number;

2. To concern themselves next with the means of establishing on solid foundations a constitution which, regulating the respective rights of the Sovereign and of the Nation, assures for each of them the greatest possible degree of strength, authority, and well-being;

3. To ask for the summoning of the Estates-General every three years; and that the laws sanctioned in it be susceptible of change or interpretation only by agreement between the authority of the King and the consent of the Nation assembled in free Estates-General;

4. To assure individual liberty and security to all citizens. This article, which aims to abolish entirely the use of *lettres de cachet* [*i.e.*, letters under signet, which contained administrative orders for imprisonment without trial or other preventive measures, sometimes in order to control the wayward sons of prominent men, sometimes for political purposes] seems to be contradicted by the frequent necessity of saving the honor of families; but this advantage cannot balance the abuses that arise from arbitrary orders of ministers; being made necessary anyway only by attainder, could it not be destroyed by enacting a law which admits to all public offices the relatives of the guilty person? Attainder is the more terrible for the Third Estate because it is the only Order that is its victim;

5. To render the ministers responsible to the Nation for abuses of their administration;

6. To establish in all the provinces freely elected Estates in which the Third Estate would have a representation equal to that of the other two Orders together;

7. To vote subsidies only after having entirely established the constitution, and to grant them only for the interval from one

session of the Estates-General to the next, unless pressing needs require imperatively a temporary aid which, in this case, would be a moderate loan;

8. To choose the simplest form for the taxes, and the one least burdensome for all classes of citizens who will pay them without discrimination;

9. To obtain an exact knowledge of the public debt, in order to sanction it and in order to adjust the subjects' sacrifices to it;

10. To ask for the reform of the laws and the courts, so that justice is rendered equally to all at the least possible cost and is located nearer the litigants;

11. To leave the deputies free to follow the dictates of their honor and conscience on the various matters which must necessarily be discussed in the Estates-General, such as the advantages to be obtained from the alienation of the royal domain, the destruction of the Concordat [of Bologna, of 1516], educational reform, chancery letters for delay of debt collection, the sale of offices and letters of nobility, which should only be the recompense for services rendered to the State, and a multitude of other abuses which are leading the kingdom to its ruin.

List of the grievances, complaints and remonstrances of the inhabitants of the parish of Saint-Jean-de-la-Ruelle, drawn up in execution of His Majesty's letters issued at Versailles on January 24, 1789

The electoral assembly, held in the church on Wednesday, February 25, was presided over by Chaufton, professor of law in the University of Orléans, in his capacity as judge of the temporal jurisdiction of the Bishop of Orléans, seigneur of the parish, de Senas d'Orgeval de Jarente. The minutes of proceedings state that there are about 100 households in the parish and list 35 men present.

1. The assembled inhabitants of the said parish complain that they pay *tailles* which are out of proportion with the

value of their lands; these are almost all only light sand planted in vines, but they pay as much per acre as the best lands of Beauce, which are in grain; yet the land of Beauce rarely fails to yield; on the contrary, in the sand of this parish barely one year out of three do the vines yield, because these lands are subject to freezing and erosion.

2. That the said inhabitants are overburdened by the *taille*, for the reason that more than half the area of the parish is possessed either by bourgeois of Orléans, who pay no *taille* for the cultivation of their vines, or by ecclesiastical property-holders having the right of mortmain, who are exempt and privileged; which makes the burden of the *taille* fall on the small number of inhabitants domiciled here.

3. The said inhabitants complain that the twentieth taxes, even as among those who pay the said twentieths, have always been badly assessed for the reason that more than a third of the area is used by strangers and persons domiciled in other parishes, the area is cut up into quarters and sixteenths of an acre and even into rods, and it is impossible for the collectors to discover the proprietors.

4. The said inhabitants say that most of them are hired vine-growers for the bourgeois of Orléans who have country houses in the said parish. As the said bourgeois pay no *taille* for the cultivation of their vines, the said hired vine-growers are taxed for the *taille* and supplements to it, in proportion to these vines they grow, so that the said hired vine-growers pay the *taille* on the property represented by their domicile and on the vines they work for hire; which amounts to an excessive burden on them that reduces them to the worst distress. The inhabitants observe that about 1774 the bourgeois of Orléans possessing vines in the parish and cultivating them themselves were taxed for the *taille;* the total assessment for the *taille* in the said parish was then increased by 400 *livres* and its supplements in proportion; several years ago, the bourgeois ceased paying the *taille;* and yet the increase established on their account has remained on the parish and has been divided among its inhabitants, which has resulted in a considerable excessive burden on them.

5. The said inhabitants therefore wish that the *taille* or any other tax established for the needs of the State may be borne

equally, in proportion to the lands possessed by each, with no exemption or privilege in favor of any person whatever.

6. The said inhabitants complain that they cannot have buildings and dwellings constructed without being subjected to the obligation called *avenage*, which consists of an annual payment to Monsieur the Duke of Orléans of a *mine* [*i.e.*, about a dozen bushels] of oats; which obligation is very burdensome and prevents the inhabitants from having any construction or dwelling on the main road.

7. The said inhabitants complain that they are subjected to the fees for masterships established in the city of Orléans, for the reason that they are in a suburb; which makes them unable to carry on the tailoring trade or keep small shops with merchandise and everyday provisions, because the fees for masterships are too considerable to allow the practice of a craft and the mediocre retail business of a few provisions in a village to be capable of making up for the payment of these fees.

8. The said inhabitants complain of being subjected to two different *corvées*, which is a duplication, to wit: the *corvées* for the Orléans and those for the road to Le Mans.

9. The said inhabitants would ask for the abolition of the *gabelle* [*i.e.*, salt-tax] and the *aides* [*i.e.*, taxes on wine] and, in case the *aides* and the *gabelle* can only be abolished one after the other, they would even ask that the *aides* be abolished first, because these taxes are still more burdensome to them than the *gabelle* and because, on the other hand, they bring in less to the State on account of the considerable costs of collection and maintenance of clerks.

10. The said inhabitants complain that about eight years ago a new roll was drawn up for the twentieth taxes on land in the said parish, by which new roll the total of the twentieths, which previously was only 1,623 *livres*, was raised to 2,672 *livres;* this increase was effected only on the basis of a few leases issued to individuals by property holders having the right of mortmain; these leases were written at too high a price, at a time when vines had risen to a great value, from which they fell off a short time afterward.

11. The said inhabitants remonstrate that the parish is only about one league [*i.e.*, two and one-half miles] long and that the parish priest's income is very moderate, since it barely amounts to a mere 250 *livres,* and it is impossible for a parish priest to live on so little; that it is desirable to raise the parish priest's income to a decent

sum sufficient to provide for his subsistence and take the endowment for this living from the income of a few simple benefices [*i.e.,* which impose no obligation to serve laymen] in the same diocese.

The present list of grievances, complaints and remonstrances was written by me, Jean-François Gramain, clerk, upon the formal request of the said inhabitants, who declared that none of them could immediately write the said list promptly enough, which has been done both from the notes brought by the said inhabitants and from the declarations they have presently made. Done on February 24, 1789, in the assembly of the said inhabitants in session before Monsieur Jean-Damien Chaufton, judge of the temporal jurisdiction of the Bishop of Orleans, on which draft the said inhabitants worked from two-thirty until five o'clock in the afternoon, and those inhabitants who know how have signed with us and those who have not signed, inquiry having been made, declared that they do not know how.

(11 signatures, including those of Chaufton and Gramain)

List of the grievances of the inhabitants of Lion-en-Sullias, in the tax district of Gien, addressed to the King of France, their sovereign lord

This village is one mile south of the Loire, halfway between Gien and Sully, and 30 miles southeast of Orléans. The seigneur was the Duke of Sully. The electoral assembly, held at the church door on Sunday, March 1, was presided over by Jean-François Arnal, one of the notaries in the town and peerage-duchy of Sully. The minutes of proceedings state that there are 55 households in the parish and list 38 men present. The occupations of 33 are mentioned: a merchant, ten cultivators of their own lands (two of these were millers as well), 22 agricultural laborers.

Let it please him to have the Estates-General assemble often, and to alleviate their woes and their misery by granting them a discharge from the obligations of the *taille, corvée, gabelle,* and twentieths, with which they are overburdened, substituting for these a single tax, territorial, in kind, at a rate in proportion to the scanty harvests they collect on their infertile ground, part of which has been absolutely worthless since the flooding of the Loire in the year 1733, while in another part of Lion the soil is rocky and shallow, a large amount of marl is needed to make it yield, and this marl costs a great deal and lasts only fifteen years.

Relying on His Majesty's paternal goodness, they dare to hope that he will accept favorably their very humble supplications and will exempt their sons and domestics from militia service in order to let them attend to the cultivation of the land and provide the kingdom with more grain, as useful to the State as military service, and they ask this with all the more reason because hands are lacking in the countryside.

What causes the countryside to be deserted is the too great misery that reigns over it, nourishment consisting only of bread made of rye most often mixed with buckwheat, curdled milk, soup usually made with a little butter and turnip oil, almost never any meat (or very rarely), a result of the extreme misery caused by the excessive burden of numerous taxes.

That another objective also is a subject of the claims of the inhabitants of the parish of Lion: the elimination of the stallions [maintained by the royal administration of stud-farms] as contrary to the perfection of the horse as a species, in that the stallions are closed in the stable all year and live only on grain and dry fodder, and they couple only with mares which live in the fields all year; there is reason to believe that the nourishing essences and those which serve for the production of the seminal fluids do not mix and unite sufficiently, since every master's first trial proves that couplings of this kind are totally null. That only too frequently the mares which are not of a size in proportion to the stallions, and even a few approaching their size, fall dead at the moment of coupling, which causes great prejudice to the proprietors and, as a necessary consequence, to the State; that before the establishment of the stallions in the Sologne, horses prospered better. Wherefore, the inhabitants of Lion beg His Majesty to be willing, by his usual goodness, to alleviate their ills by diminishing their misery and to receive the assurance of their love, submission, and fidelity.

The inhabitants of Lion also beg His Majesty to abolish *francs-fiefs* as contrary and hindering to trade and to permit them to reimburse at a decent rate all land, rents, and dues owed to laymen and ecclesiastics.

Done and adopted at Lion-on-the-Ronce, on March 1, 1789.
(Six signatures, including that of Arnal)

List of the grievances, complaints, and remonstrances of the inhabitants of the parish of Pithiviers-le-Vieil

This village is two miles west of the town of Pithiviers and 25 miles northeast of Orléans. Its seigneur was the Bishop of Orléans. The electoral assembly, held at the warden's stall in the church on Sunday, March 1, was presided over by Denis-Bernard Pointeau, prosecutor and attorney representing the Bishop in the seigneurial court of Pithiviers. The minutes of proceedings state that there are 160 households in the parish and list 67 men present, of whom 10 are identified as cultivators of their own lands.

1. Full of confidence that the King is assembling the Nation to bring about the general welfare of the kingdom in all possible ways, the said inhabitants will charge their deputies to the Estates-General to ask for the general list of the receipts and expenditures of the kingdom to serve as the basis of their work.

2. Next they will ask for the elimination of all useless expenditures in all parts of the administration, after which they will consent to all those for the dignity of the throne, the glory and the prosperity of the State.

3. To provide for all these expenses and also succeed in reducing certain taxes which are crushing the countryside, the deputies will be charged to ask that all taxes generally, of whatever sort, be paid equally by the three orders—that is, by the Clergy, the Nobility, and the Third Estate, the said inhabitants being certain that if everyone contributes in proportion to his capacity, receipts will exceed expenditures.

4. The deputies will strongly emphasize that there be only one form of taxation and only one assessment roll for the three orders.

5. The deputies will then be able to make it known that the *taille* and the taxes supplementary to it are desolating the countryside and arresting the progress of agriculture and that if this tax cannot at once be entirely suppressed, it should at least be reduced,

having regard for the capacity of those who pay it, their efforts and difficulties and the risks they run because of the accidents that often afflict the countryside.

6. It ought to be the same for the salt tax. This tax is more of a burden to the countryside because the consumption of salt is greater than in the towns, in view of the nature of the daily diet and the number of animals for which this substance is useful. If the condition of the finances of the kingdom does not permit entirely abolishing this tax, at least it ought to be reduced to half of the excessive price at which salt is fixed.

7. Ask for the conversion of the *champart,* exorbitant by its nature, into a money payment, fixed by the acre and not susceptible of increase or decrease on the pretext of a change in the crop being cultivated, liberty to accomplish this being inherent in the right of property.

8. Order of Malta [*i.e.,* the Knights of the Order of Saint John of Jerusalem]. This order enjoys prerogatives that are extremely burdensome. The leases let by one of its commanderies expire on the day a commander retires. It seems to be excepted from all the laws; when the harvest has begun and the grain is almost all stored, the Order takes it, and while paying merely for tillage and for hired labor and seeds, it takes the cultivator's hope, his resource, the fruit of his work, and leaves him its burdens. Such is the jurisprudence of the Great Council [the highest royal court that adjudicated disputes over ecclesiastical property], exorbitant, contrary to the rights of the Nation, and ruinous for cultivators. The Third Estate hopes that the abolition of these rights will be expressly solicited.

9. And, if proceedings are begun to reform the civil and criminal laws, ask that those substituted for the old laws be drawn up in such a way as to place the life, the honor, the liberty, and the property of subjects under the ceaseless protection of these new laws, which will have clarity and simplicity adequate to make them easily understood and executed.

10. The delays and costs of justice are truly a scourge for country people. In consequence, it will be proper to fix time limits, within which cases must be terminated, and costs which they cannot exceed, having regard for the order of jurisdictions and the objects at issue.

11. It would be of great advantage both for the King and for the people if the collection of certain taxes was simplified by abolishing the obscure financial code, a labyrinth in which one loses one's way; these taxes, like the salt tax, are consumed by the profits of tax farming and administration, and the payments to the King's treasury have absolutely no proportion to the sums drawn from the people: such are the *aides, contrôles, insinuations, centième denier, amortissements, francs-fiefs*, etc.

12. The right of hunting is devastating our countrysides. We do not ask that it be abolished, but that our grain be protected by law from all the wrongs and damage suffered by cultivators from the gamekeepers and the excessive quantity of game and that hunting be prohibited when our grain is on the stalks. Nothing causes more ravages than the hare. It takes away the cultivator's hope for a harvest, leaving him unable to obtain compensation except by paying fees which make the lawsuit more costly than profitable for him.

13. The dovecots are too numerous; the seigneurs of simple fiefs [*i.e.*, with no dependent estates] claim to have the right to them, and the multitude of pigeons work frightful destruction on the grain, especially on the early shoots; in order to oblige the seigneurs to feed their pigeons, at least let individuals be permitted to kill them when they find them devastating their fields.

14. There is a river that runs through the parish for a distance of a league and a half whose flow is impeded by mills which in the upper reaches (not having a steep enough slope) can turn only with accumulations of water: this ruins all the meadows, which are no longer of any use, consisting only of small shrubs and reeds. Add to this the bad air that occasions fevers every year and putridity [*i.e.*, typhoid] from time to time, which wipes out many people.

15. That the militia be abolished. It depopulates our countryside. The young men who are required to draw lots are nearly all from the most indigent class of citizens. The parents of these unfortunates join together with the greatest sorrow and even with tears to make up a purse to indemnify the one who loses in the drawing; these sums of money too often deprive unfortunate families of their very subsistence.

16. That all the orders of the State be subject to the *corvée*, and that the money from this tax be put into a treasury and used in

each tax district for road maintenance and charitable work, and that it be prohibited to remove any of these funds from one tax district to another.

17. That it is in order for His Majesty, having established provincial assemblies in the provinces with *élections* [*i.e.*, tax districts], divided into departments and municipalities, to grant the said municipalities a sort of police jurisdiction, to control wine shops which provide drinks during divine service and at late hours, to watch the beggars and vagabonds, and to cause the arrest of disturbers of the public peace.

18. That if the casual fees, which the parish priests customarily collect, are abolished, the income of the living of Pithiviers-le-Vieil would be too small for so demanding a parish, composed of 160 households in 14 localities at distances of half or three-quarters of a league from the church; that this income can be increased by giving the parish priest all the tithes which, although mere alms, are in the hands of ecclesiastical superiors.

(45 signatures, including that of Pointeau)

List of complaints and grievances proposed for the Estates-General by the inhabitants of Erceville, in the bailliage of Orléans

This village is five miles northeast of Toury and 25 miles north of Orléans. Its name was spelled Arceville in the eighteenth century. The seigneur was Rolland, presiding judge of the *chambre des requêtes du palais* in the Parlement of Paris. The electoral assembly, held in the local courtroom on Tuesday, March 3, was presided over by the seigneurial judge, Jean-Charles Petit. The minutes of proceedings state that there are 69 households in the parish and list 22 men present, mentioning their occupations: seven cultivators of their own lands, two wineshop-keepers (one of these was also a tailor), four masons and roof-thatchers, four agricultural laborers, a farrier, a cartwright, a carter, a herdsman, and a vigneron.

The said inhabitants hope that the goodness of the King, in whom they put all their confidence, and the enlightenment of the Estates-General will reform the abuses which have crept into the finances up to the present time, so that the money collected from them no longer passes through so many hands, in which it is diminished, but goes directly to the treasury to provide for the needs of the State, to which they are always ready to contribute, like His Majesty's other subjects; and as it is with confidence that they hope for the reform of abuses, they propose their particular grievances as follows:

1. The said inhabitants observe that they alone have been charged with the mass of the taxes, while their seigneur, who farms much of the land in the parish, enjoys total exemption, although he has had a great part of the land planted with woods, which are populated by game that devastates the rest of the countryside; and that the woods, as well as the avenues he has had planted in great quantity, damage and almost destroy the neighboring lands, so that these lands, even in the better years, yield no harvest. Wherefore they ask that, concurrently with them and without any distinction of title or rank, the said seigneur be taxed like them, as well as all the other seigneurs who possess property in this parish, in proportion to their property together with their avenues and lands adjacent to the latter up to 50 feet from the said woods and avenues, and that everyone be permitted to destroy the game which ruins his crop.

2. They complain that the tithe and the *champart* take a large part of the compost from their lands, so that, far from being able to improve their lands, they sadly watch them deteriorate annually through the removal of straw and fodder that would serve not only for the enrichment of their lands but also for the nourishment of their cattle. Wherefore they ask that the tithe and the *champart* be abolished, or at least converted into an annual payment in money.

3. That in this province there is a tax that perhaps does not exist elsewhere, which is the tax on importation and exportation of wine, the source of innumerable legal proceedings begun by the employes of the administration. Wherefore they petition that the said tax on wines and other drinks be abolished as to importation, or at least made similar to those in the other provinces of the kingdom.

4. The [payment known as] *franc fief* was established to prevent commoners from possessing noble fiefs, and "noble fiefs" should refer only to seigneurial lands with vassals and land-holders paying

the [rent known as] *cens* dependent on them, not lands belonging to seigneurs which are merely simple subordinate fiefs; moreover, this burdensome payment is required at every transfer of ownership, not merely upon direct inheritance, with the 50 per cent supplement, so that it often happens that a proprietor of this sort of property pays three years' worth of income from his property in two consecutive years, without any deduction from the other taxes due on it; and, considering that the said tax is a badge of servitude abhorred by a free people, they ask for its entire abolition.

5. The said inhabitants observe that they pay an infinity of taxes although knowing neither their origin nor the laws in virtue of which they pay them: among others, a tax of one per cent on the stipulated value of the rings and jewels provided for the bride in a marriage contract; a tax which was never asked for, which has only been required for about six months, and which occasions scandalous investigations into all the marriage contracts in the last twenty years and more. Wherefore they petition that all the taxes be abolished which presently exist and were not consented to by the Nation assembled, notwithstanding every verification and registration by the courts [*i.e.*, the parlements] which were not empowered to consent; and that in the future no tax can be established, either permanently or temporarily, without the consent of the whole Nation assembled in Estates-General.

As for the rest, the said inhabitants declare that they leave it to what is to be decided in the assembly of the Estates-General.

Done and adopted in the general assembly of all the inhabitants of the said parish of Arceville, this day, March 3, 1789.

(14 signatures, including that of Petit)

Part Two

THE FALL OF THE BASTILLE AND THE WOMEN'S MARCH TO VERSAILLES, 1789

The Bastille, in ordinary times, was chiefly used as a royal state prison. Its historic role in earlier periods of crisis and uprisings had been to surrender, without a fight, to the city of Paris. In 1789, its capture was a revolutionary event of symbolic importance.

The event was preceded by a worsening shortage of bread; by episodes of violence on a small scale for limited purposes; by a great increase in the number of royal troops in the Paris area, leading to a protest from the National Assembly against the troop concentrations; and by growing suspicions that the King and his council intended to disperse the National Assembly and revert to an authoritative policy. On July 11, the finance minister Necker was dismissed, and the King's chief military adviser, Marshal de Broglie, wrote to Besenval, commander in Paris: "If there is a general outbreak, limit the plan of defense to the Bourse, the Royal Treasury, the Bastille, and the Hôtel des Invalides," that is, to the great financial institutions and the most defensible military establishments. On July 13, the electors of Paris, who had chosen the commoners' deputies from the city to the Estates-General, reassembled to transform themselves into a provisional municipal government and to organize a bourgeois militia, later to become the National Guard.

The Attackers

On the morning of July 14, a large crowd invaded the Hôtel des Invalides, which was a storehouse of weapons as well as a barracks for old soldiers. "Arriving pell-mell on the esplanade, they presented an order from the city hall to the Governor [of the Hôtel des Invalides] to turn over the arms, and he, seeing no way of defending the Hôtel, opened its doors." So reported an eyewitness, Besenval's nephew, Salmour. The crowd made off with 30,000 muskets.

On the same morning, representatives of the assembly of electors of Paris went from the city hall to the Bastille. Discussions with the commandant did not succeed in eliminating misunderstanding and were superseded by violence.

Ten days later, Louis-Abel Beffroy de Reigny, editor of the fortnightly *Courrier des Planètes* and a minor playwright and versifier, wrote a pamphlet, *Précis exact de la prise de la Bastille,* translated here with a few omissions.

Amidst the troubles inseparable from the extraordinary events which have just taken place, there have been so many different versions of the details that the public has at first been but very imperfectly informed of the truth. This is the exact account of the circumstances that preceded, accompanied, and followed the fall of the Bastille. Posterity will scarcely believe that memorable revolution if authentic and detailed writings do not perpetuate the memory of it and serve as an immortal monument which consecrates that stroke of magnanimity. Several persons have been parading a bravery that has been uncontested while the facts have not been carefully collected. Let us listen only to the truth and neglect to mention none of the glorious names which, in this incredible event, have a public right to our homage.

On Tuesday, July 14, 1789, a detachment of grenadiers of Ruffé-ville and a detachment of fusiliers of the Lubersac company had been planning an attack on the Bastille since one o'clock and were occupied in collecting the equipment for it when about three o'clock a bourgeois named Hulin, manager of [the laundry called] the Buanderie de la Reine at La Briche, near Saint-Denis, appeared and said to them: "My friends, are you Citizens? Of course you are. Let's march to the Bastille; they're slaughtering the bourgeois and your comrades; both are your brothers. Will you let them to be the victims of the most cruel betrayal?"

At these words, the French Guards, who had not been waiting for this new encouragement, since they were already prepared to leave, set off under the command of Wargnier, sergeant-major of grenadiers, and Labarthe, sergeant of grenadiers, with a zeal and an ardor worthy of the courage they had already shown on so many occasions. They were followed by a certain number of Citizens, joined by many others as they went.

They took the route by way of the Port au Blé, the French Guards commanded by their sergeants and the bourgeois by Hulin. . . .

They had with them three cannon, to which were added two other pieces they came across near the Arsenal.

Without difficulty they entered the first court on the Celestins' side; there they found a few Invalides soldiers, who had surrendered their arms in the morning and who joined the besiegers. From there, they entered the second court without trouble, and so on into the courts of the Bastille.

The action began at the entrance of the Salpêtres court where they placed a cannon, which they discharged only once, after the grenadiers and fusiliers had fired from line.

They crossed the court after the French Guards and the bourgeois had fired several more times and reached the second arch.

There the cannon was aimed again, and they took the Invalides' barrack, from which they fired at the openings in the fortress, to prevent maneuvers by the enemy.

Let us not forget to name Élie, officer of the Queen's Infantry regiment, who boldly crossed the line of fire and got the wagons of manure overturned which had been put at the entrance of the second court to block the passage to the besiegers.

Then, with cannon shot, the chains of the drawbridge were cut, to prevent a betrayal; it was Hulin who first advised this necessary expedient.

The manure spilled from the wagons had been set on fire, and this fire was very favorable to the besiegers, because of the thick smoke which obscured the maneuvers of the soldiers and bourgeois.

A poor Invalides soldier, having gone to seek refreshments for the besiegers, became the victim of his zeal and perished a few steps from the blaze.

The enemies were firing more vigorously then; the besiegers passed into the last court, despite the danger, which frightened no one, and reached the bridge that led immediately into the fortress.

The enemies' fire had lasted nearly two hours, when the white flag was raised from the top of the Basinière tower, the first on the left as one enters from the southern side.

Hulin had taken the precaution to tell six grenadiers to go on the battlements of the drawbridge of the fortress.

Then the enemy, seeing that the white flag he had raised had inspired no greater confidence in the Citizens and the Soldiers, who were continuing to fire, took the course of presenting himself behind the drawbridge and passed through the slits a paper that could not be read because of the distance. An unidentified individual went to find a plank, by means of which it would be possible to approach the paper. This unfortunate, another victim of his own zeal, fell into the ditch and lost his life.

At this instant, Maillard, whose father is a mounted bailiff at the [law-court entitled] Châtelet of Paris, had the courage to retrieve the paper and put it in the hands of Hulin and the other chiefs who, together with all the besiegers who could get a look at it, read these words: "We have twenty thousand rounds of powder, and we will blow up the garrison and you too if you do not accept the capitulation."

This threat did not have the effect that was expected of it. The besiegers shot at the drawbridge; three cannon were brought forward and discharged at the bridge.

The enemy, seeing that they were attempting to destroy the bridge, let down the small drawbridge on the left of the entrance into the fortress.

Despite the new danger arising from this maneuver by the enemy, Élie, Hulin, and Maillard jumped on the small bridge and shouted for the last gate to be opened.

The French Guards, remaining cool amid the peril, formed a barrier on the other side of the bridge to prevent the crowd of besiegers from collecting there. This act of prudence, in the heat of the action, ought to be mentioned; for without this precaution, thousands of persons would have lost their lives.

Then the gate was opened; Élie entered first and the others afterward, without anyone experiencing the least accident.

Everyone having entered the great court in the fortress, which forms a rectangle 120 feet long by 80 feet wide, Maillard, who knew the governor, began by seizing him, calling for help, because the great drawbridge was being lowered. A grenadier named Arné came running and, taking hold of the governor together with Maillard, put him in the hands of Hulin and Élie.

M. de Launey was carrying a stick with a gold head and sword point, with which he tried to pierce his own breast; Arné wrested it from him.

The People continuing to demand confusedly a prompt death for the governor, the two persons who had taken him sought to preserve him from the fury; they led him outside and to the square in front of the city hall [the Place de Grève], not without sharing the ill treatment that their prisoner experienced.

Everyone knows the fate of that unfortunate officer, whose tragic end caused a sensation which will last as long as that action is remembered.

Such are the exact details of the taking of the Bastille. All France resounded with this stroke of valor; our children will recount it to our last descendants, and the foreigner who learns of it will know the worth of the Parisians.

Citizen Monarch! Sensitive and loyal man! Cherished King of all virtuous Frenchmen! Oh, Louis XVI! You have seen what your faithful subjects can do in their own defense; you have seen what they will be able to do in yours whenever you approach them with the confidence of a father. They love you, they revere you, and only await your heart's desire to seal it with their blood.

> En tremblant pour lui-même, il pensait à son Roi,
> Et son dernière soupir aurait été pour toi.

And you, the Nation's brave soldiers, whom a blind fury seemed to be arming against your brothers, from the recital of this memorable action you will learn to admire them, to cherish them; and your courageous hands will no longer aim their strokes against any but enemy nations.

We cannot too much admire the bravery and intrepidity of the French Guards, who, under the leadership of MM. Wargnier and Labarthe, in a two-and-a-half-hour siege, gave as many proofs of valor as one sees in the history of the most famous sieges. Here are the names of the soldiers who contributed to this success; we do not name the Bourgeois, because it would be impossible to identify them all.

List of the French Guards in the Detachment at the Bastille, July 14, 1789
[63 names]

Important Addition

When this summary was drawn up, Élie, officer in the Queen's Infantry regiment, was absent; what is said about him was dictated by the other persons present, who cited only what they had observed in the heat of the action. It is probable that amidst an expedition of this nature, which required enthusiasm and quickness, each of the besiegers, occupied with his personal danger and the purpose he was trying to achieve, was not able to notice carefully what was happening to his right and left. Élie, having learned that the author had been asked to write this relation, came to find him and told him of details which had escaped the others. Élie is the less suspect in that he showed distinction throughout, was borne in triumph and crowned at the city hall, was offered as a recompense the silver from the Bastille, which he generously refused. . . . Here are the details and the corrections that were lacking in this summary:

It was Élie who received the capitulation, because he was the first one on the small bridge; he has it still and has shown it to the author. It is conceived in these terms: "We have twenty thousand rounds of powder, and we will blow up the garrison and the whole quarter if you do not accept the capitulation."

. . . Maillard, who was carrying the flag, turned it over to other hands and went on the plank to get the paper, which he turned over to Élie. This act of bravery is the more astonishing in that an unfortunate, all in rags, had had the courage to risk the attempt and had been killed.

. . . M. de Launey was in the court of the fortress when the crowd entered there; he had on a short grey-white frock coat, no hat, no Cross of Saint Louis but only a ribbon, like an officer in undress uniform. In the same court were about thirty Swiss and a Swiss officer at their head.

. . . P.S. If this recital still lacks essential particulars, the author is to be excused for not recounting them, because he has not been informed of them. He believes himself obliged to declare that he was not in the expedition to the Bastille because his work on his periodical and the weakness of his health kept him at home, that he shared the alarms and sentiments of all good citizens, that chance dictated his selection to draw up this narrative, . . . that he has done it without compromising anyone. . . . His first concern has always been and will always be not to depart from the limits of prudence; and he declares that he has never received a *sou* from this sort of productions.

The Besieged

The rumors that circulated immediately after July 14 and the multiplication of published accounts by persons who claimed to have been eyewitnesses tended to present the garrison soldiers in an unfavorable light. Some of them sought to defend their probity, bravery, and patriotism by preparing a memorandum, which they turned over to the editor of a publication devoted to the history of the Bastille.

In the second installment of this publication, which appeared in early September, 1789, the names of the seven prisoners who were in the Bastille are listed, and the defensive preparations that had been taken are described. On the towers there were eleven cannon capable of firing eight-pound balls, four cannon firing four-pound balls, mounted on marine gun carriages which could not readily be moved back for reloading and were ordinarily used merely for salutes. In the great court, facing the entrance, were three field cannon loaded with grapeshot and a rampart-musket capable of firing one-and-a-half pound balls. The garrison had 15,000 cartridges and 56,000 pounds of powder. Its provisions consisted of two sacks of flour and some rice, a certain amount of wood, but no oven except a small pastry oven; above all, the water supply was dependent on pipes from a basin outside.

The account, omitting the anonymous editor's footnotes, continues as follows, from *La Bastille dévoilée, ou Recueil de pièces authentiques pour servir à son histoire,* 2ᵉ livraison, pp. 87-113.

The garrison was composed of 32 soldiers of the Salis-Samade regiment, commanded by M. Louis de Flue, lieutenant of grenadiers; of 82 Invalides soldiers, of whom two were cannoneers from the Monsigny company; they are presently, as we have already said, at the Hôtel des Invalides, in Sainte-Croix ward. It is they who gave us all the notes we have just reported and the memorandum that follows, which we are going to copy literally.

On July 12, the revolution began in Paris. About seven o'clock in the evening, people assembled in different sections and took up arms.

On the 13th, at two o'clock in the morning, M. de Launey had the company take up arms and come back inside, the company and the 32 Swiss who had been at the Bastille since a few days before. He had the gates closed that lead to their barracks, where the company had left all its effects. . . .

The garrison remained in the interior of the Bastille all day on the 13th. Sentries were placed everywhere the governor thought them necessary, and twelve men were commanded to climb up on the towers, in order to observe what was happening outside. . . .

On the 14th, at ten o'clock in the morning, three individuals came to the main gate of the Bastille and told the soldier who was there that they wanted to speak to the governor, that they were deputies from the city hall. The soldier conducted them to the small drawbridge of the outworks, and caused the governor to be told that three deputies from the city hall, accompanied by a great multitude, were asking for him. The governor and the other officers of the command presented themselves at the first bridge and had it lowered. But the governor, seeing the immense crowd which was following these deputies, told them that only three could enter and that he was going to send out as hostages four fusiliers who would remain with the people until the moment when the three deputies would leave the Bastille. The four fusiliers went out, and the three deputies were brought in. They were still in the governor's office when M. [Thuriot] de la Rosière entered, likewise followed by many individuals of all classes, who stopped in the first court, opposite the bridge from the outworks. As soon as the first three deputies had gone out, M. de la Rosière spoke to M. de Launey. . . .

M. de la Rosière asked the governor for permission to enter the inner court; M. de Launey granted it, but reluctantly and in accordance with the request that he do so made by M. de Losme, major. Having entered, M. de la Rosière urged the officers and soldiers whom he found there, in the name of honor, of the nation, and of the Patrie, to change the direction of the cannon and to surrender. At the suggestion of the governor himself, the officers and soldiers swore that they would not fire and would not use their arms if no one attacked them.

M. de la Rosière then asked and obtained from the governor permission to go up on the towers to see everything for himself and to be in a position to render a more faithful account of his mission to the citizens who had sent him. Having come down with the governor, he said in a loud voice, in the presence of the officers and company in the court, that he was content, that he was going to make his report to the people, that he was hoping they would not refuse to provide a bourgeois guard to guard the Bastille together with the troops who were there. He left the fort and went with M. de Launey back to the governor's office. The people, impatient at not seeing their deputy return, shouted for him. At once, M. de la Rosière appeared at a window and calmed them by telling them that in an instant he was going to join them. In fact, a few minutes afterward he went out.

But merely a half-hour later, what was the commanding officers' surprise, and ours, to see the people arrive in a crowd, armed with muskets, sabers, swords, hatchets, etc., and shouting, "We want the Bastille; down with the troops," addressing the soldiers who were on the towers. As decently as possible we begged these various individuals to withdraw, and we tried to acquaint them with the danger to which they were exposing themselves.

Despite our representations, the people were obstinate. Two men climbed up on the roof of the guard-house, which was beside the small drawbridge, cut and broke with hatchet blows the chains of the big bridge while others chopped and smashed those of the small one, which obliged us to tell them firmly to withdraw or we would really be forced to fire on them. They succeeded in lowering the big and little bridges of the outworks. Emboldened by this success, they ran in a crowd to the second bridge, in order to take it, firing muskets at the troops.

We were forced to fire on them to prevent them from forcibly lowering the second bridge, as they had the first. . . .

An hour after this attack there was heard, from the Arsenal side, the noise of a drum, accompanied by terrible shouts. At once we saw a flag escorted by an immense crowd of armed citizens. This flag remained in the Elm court with the smaller portion of the troop who had accompanied it; the more considerable number advanced into the Government court, shouting to us not to fire, that they were deputies from the city hall who wanted to speak to the governor, whom they begged to descend. M. de Launey and the fusiliers who were then on the towers shouted to them to send forward the flag and the deputies from the city hall, and to get the people to withdraw into the Passageway court. At the same instant a fusilier named Guyot de Fléville, to prove to them that our intention was not to fire on them, turned his musket barrel downward, butt upward, and urged us to imitate him, which we did immediately. . . .

After many requests from the Invalides soldiers, the people stopped, and the deputies came through the wooden door into the Passageway court, where they must have seen all the soldiers on the towers, the butts of their muskets upward, who shouted to them to enter with their flag to speak to the governor, giving their word of honor that they would not fire on them. The deputies must likewise have seen on the platform a white flag as a sign of peace.

The deputies remained in that court about ten minutes without being willing to come forward to speak to the governor, despite the promise of the fusiliers, who were shouting to them from the tops of the towers. . . .

Without listening to their proposals, the deputies withdrew into the Elm court, where they remained more than a quarter of an hour, either to consult each other or to listen to what we continued to shout to them, not to go away, that the Bastille would be turned over to them if they were truly deputies from the city hall.

The governor said to us: "You must see, Messieurs, that these deputies and this flag are not from the city hall; it is surely a flag which the people have taken and are using to surprise us. If they were really deputies, they would not have hesitated, after the promises you made to them, to come and inform me of the intentions of the city hall."

The deputies remained no more than a quarter of an hour in the Elm court; they left, taking with them a very small part of the persons who had accompanied them. The larger part remained, and filled the three courts—the Elm, the Passageway, and the Government. The deputies having left, the people went in a crowd to attack the second bridge, resolved to lower it by force like the first. The fusiliers on the towers shouted to the assailants not to advance, that they were going to be fired on; but they would not listen to anything. From their shouts and fierce determination, the company thought that the deputies who had just presented themselves were not deputies from the city hall. The governor gave the order to fire: this discharge scattered them, and several remained on the ground. . . .

An hour later, they brought three wagons of straw and set fire to the guard-house in the outworks, to the Government, and to the kitchens. It was at this moment that a cannon discharged grapeshot, the only cannonshot from the Bastille during the combat, which lasted five hours. The defense used only muskets. Whatever advantage was expected from the fire, it was more prejudicial than useful to the besiegers, and, far from making the Bastille easier to take, served to defend it and to render the second bridge unapproachable.

It was then that we saw the French Guards appear and place in the Elm court two four-pounders: a cannon decorated with silver, from the Wardrobe, and a mortar. They also placed two pieces at the gate which leads to the garden of the Arsenal. Since the surrender of the fort, we have been assured that these pieces, before being where we saw them, had been placed near Lesdiguières passage and Guemenée cul-de-sac. . . .

We must not forget to cite Férand and Bécard, who saved the city of Paris from the greatest of misfortunes. About four o'clock, the governor, urged by the fusiliers to surrender the Bastille, himself seeing that he could no longer sustain the siege, lacking food, took the fuse from one of the cannon in the inner court to set fire to the powder which was in the Liberté tower, which would unfailingly have blown up part of the faubourg Saint-Antoine, and all the houses neighboring the Bastille, if these two fusiliers had not prevented the execution of his design; they pointed bayonets at him and forced him back from the powder supply. . . .

It was then that M. de Launey asked the garrison what course of action to take, [saying] that he saw nothing to do but blow ourselves up rather than be slaughtered by the people, whose fury was inescapable, that we must go back up on the towers, continue to fight, and blow ourselves up rather than surrender.

The soldiers answered him that it was impossible to fight any longer, that they were resigned to anything rather than to cause so many citizens to perish, that it was more in order to have the drummer climb up on the towers to beat Retreat, to raise a white flag, and to capitulate. The governor, not having a flag, gave them a white handkerchief. Rousse and Roulard climbed up on the towers, raised the flag, went three times around the platform with the drum beating Retreat, which lasted about a quarter of an hour; the people were firing continuously without paying attention to the flag or the Retreat.

A quarter of an hour after the Invalides soldiers and the drummer had come down, the besiegers, seeing that no one was firing any longer from any part of the Bastille, advanced, still firing, to the inner bridge shouting, "Lower the bridge!" The Swiss officer addressed them through a kind of loophole which was located next to the drawbridge and asked to come out with the honors of war; they refused. The said officer wrote the capitulation and passed it through the same opening, saying that we wanted to surrender and lay down arms if they promised not to massacre the troops; they began to shout: "Lower your bridge; nothing will happen to you."

On this promise, the governor gave the key of the small drawbridge, which he had in his pocket, to Guillard, corporal, and Piroux, fusilier, who opened the door and lowered the bridge. It is certain that if it had been foreseen what was going to happen, the bridge would have been lowered only after a regular, written capitulation signed by the city hall.

The door was no sooner opened than the people rushed into the court and threw themselves on the Invalides, who had deposited their arms along the wall on the right on entering. The Swiss were on the other side, but they escaped this first movement; wearing smocks, they were mistaken for prisoners. Besides, they had not been seen; they had not climbed up on the towers; they were in the court, where they had been firing continuously, both through the loopholes and through holes they had made in the drawbridge.

The people were so blinded that they went in a crowd into the commanding officers' lodging, broke the furniture inside, the doors, and the windows. During this time, citizens who were in the court were shouting at these same citizens, whom they mistook for men of the garrison; several of them were killed.

The Invalides were led like slaves into several places in Paris; twenty-two were taken to the city hall. After humiliations and torments of all kinds, they saw, on arriving there, two of their comrades hanged. . . . Voices arose from all parts of the square shouting "Give them to us, let's hang them." At once some French Guards asked for mercy for us, and the people, returned to their senses, granted it to us. We rested about a half-hour, and the French Guards themselves escorted us to . . . one of their barracks.

It is easy to see that the Bastille was not taken by assault. No breach was made; we defy anyone whatever to prove otherwise. They entered when we had the bridge lowered, and M. Élie was the first soldier we saw in the court.

The Invalides are aware of all that is imputed to them; perhaps people will change their minds when they know the unfortunate circumstances in which they found themselves. If they had resisted the orders of the governor any longer, they were to be shot by the Swiss. It would therefore have been necessary for them to shoot the Swiss and to drench their hands in the blood of the officers commanding them.

The Invalides lost all that they possessed; their quarters were entirely devastated.

The garrison lost only one man during the combat, the one called Fortuné, shot dead on the towers. Three or four Invalides soldiers were slightly wounded.

List of the Persons Killed or Wounded After the Reduction of the Place

M. de Launey, governor, decapitated at the Place de Grève;

M. de Losme de Salbray, major, killed at the Place de Grève, opposite the Arcade Saint-Jean;

M. Miray, aide-major, killed on Rue des Tournelles;

M. Person, lieutenant of the company, killed at the Port aux Blés;

M. Caron, lieutenant of the company, wounded in four places [since recovered];

Dumont, Invalides soldier, attacked by the crowd in the fort, died the following night;

Asselin and Bécard, hanged at the Place de Grève.

Here ends the memorandum and the information supplied by the Invalides soldiers. . . .

"When Shall We Have Bread?"

While the National Assembly began debate on a new constitution, and the peasants in parts of the country experienced the panic and disorder known as the Great Fear, the population in Paris continued to have difficulty obtaining food. The atmosphere in some sections of the capital emerges clearly from the pages of a pamphlet published at the end of September.

Excerpts follow, from *Quand aurons-nous du pain? Vous dormez, Parisiens, et vous manquez de pain!*

Go, keen expression of my rightful anguish, go and carry desolation and despair into all hearts if the Parisians do not have the courage to throw off the yoke of the tyrants, of the monopolists, who are oppressing them and causing them to die of hunger.

All kinds of governments, says Livy, are scrupulous to see that the citizens never lack food; the tranquillity of the State depends on it. A starved people is easily moved to excesses. But everyone knows the gentleness of the Restorers of French Liberty.

Why, Citizens, do La Fayette, Bailly, and the chiefs of the Commune leave you in want of BREAD? It is in order to grow fat at the expense of your substance.

Why do those villains bring troops to encircle Paris, Versailles, and the surrounding area with pikes and soldiers, on the pretext of guarding the King and the National Assembly?

It is to have the means of starving you and weakening you within a couple of days, in order to be able to slaughter you with no risk. But open your eyes: when shall we have BREAD?

You know that the King has come alone into your midst. You

know that the King and the National Assembly were safe when
you made sacrifices to the Patrie of Berthier, Foulon, De Launey,
etc., etc. Now you are silent, and you are dying of hunger. . . .

The chiefs of your Committees are doing everything. They scorn
the regulations and observations of the general Assembly of each
District, . . . and you are asleep, and you do not have BREAD.

As the other Committees will not perhaps be so easy to corrupt,
La Fayette reserves for himself the right to name your Military
Chiefs. Ask him, then, when shall we have BREAD? . . .

You want to provide Ministers for the King, you want to name
the Generals, you want them to account to the Nation; but you
throw yourselves into the arms of La Fayette, you give him a
despotic power over you, you make him master of everything. Your
life is safer, then, in the hands of that betrayer, La Fayette, of that
Vampire, than in those of your good King: admit that you are
fools, for you do not have BREAD.

How much does bread cost? a foreigner lately asked a workman's
wife. Three *livres* and twelve *sous* for four pounds, she replied.
What, he said, that is eighteen *sous* a pound! Yes, she said, it is
fixed at twelve *sous* for four pounds, but one cannot get any. My
husband has to spend an entire day at a baker's door to get a
poor loaf weighing four pounds. He earns three *livres* a day, but
not being able to work for lack of bread he loses his wages of
three *livres,* so the bread comes to three *livres* and twelve *sous* for
four pounds. Alas! When shall we have BREAD?

It used to be permitted to go into the Market; it is to the Market
that they are supposed to transport the flour. What does the
Cannibal Committee do? It prohibits the Bourgeois from entering
the Market to keep them from seeing the infamies that are committed there. It sends the bakers to look for flour outside Paris,
that is to say, in places where there is none because it has been
secretly exported. Thus the poor baker is obliged to cheat you of
one pound on each four-pound loaf. But when shall we have BREAD?

The Committee gives out that indiscreet Bourgeois have gone
into the storage rooms in the Market where there is spoiled flour
unfit for human consumption which is not even sold to the paper-
hangers. What do they do with this if they do not sell it? Why
not throw it in the river? They keep it, but for what use if not to
mix it with other flour to be eaten by the silly Parisians? Poor

simpletons, you admire your chiefs, you are asleep. But when shall we have BREAD?

The Subsistence Committee sends Commissioners at great expense to buy flour in the provincial towns. The Petits Augustins District was assigned Brie, and in four or five days it performed prodigies, was well received by all the Farm stewards, from whom it brought eighty wagons to the Market.

The other Commissioners, thinking themselves Farmers-General of the Ovens, have amused themselves by giving dinners, and after more than a month had only five or six wagons of flour brought to the Market. Yet the Parisians are seeing their capitation tax increased; enormous expenses are counted as theirs; and we lack food. When shall we have BREAD?

More than a third of the inhabitants of the Capital are away; Heaven has poured its benefits profusely on our soil; the harvest has been very abundant; we should be overflowing with flour, and we have no bread. The Subsistence Committee's posters promise us food; it says it is sweating blood to go far and wide in search of flour; but hunger is pressing us; we are beginning to see that these unfulfilled promises are made only with the intention of deceiving us. They give us bread only in writing; when shall we have some in substance?

Although the grumbling of our intestines makes us aware that we are experiencing the horrors of need, they want to persuade us that our stomachs are full when they are empty, when we lack the food most precious to life. This will continue, and when shall we have BREAD? . . .

A Letter from Versailles

The events in Versailles on October 5 and 6 provided the first opportunity for many in the royal entourage and the National Assembly to observe a Paris crowd in action and made a deeper impression than even the fall of the Bastille had done. This is reflected in the following letter, from Guy Le Gentil, marquis de Paroy, to his wife. He was 61 years old and was military commander in the province of Champagne, where he was elected deputy to the

Estates-General for the nobility of Provins. His wife was the sister of Louis-Philippe de Rigaud, marquis de Vaudreuil, 65 years old, a lieutenant-general in the royal navy and deputy to the Estates-General for the nobility of Castelnaudary.
This letter was published in the *Revue de la Révolution*, I (1883) Documents, 1-7.

Versailles
October 6, 1789
five o'clock in the afternoon

My dear,

I can imagine your anxiety, and so I hasten to dispel your uneasiness concerning me. I do not know, however, whether I have the strength to recount to you this fatal day, I am still so affected by the events I have just witnessed. I am still alive, but I really thought, when I arose this morning, that this would be the last day of my life.

I am going to begin my account at the moment when I left you yesterday at eight o'clock in the morning. You know that they came to tell me a great assemblage of people had formed in the faubourgs and at the Place de Grève. I thought I had not a moment to lose to regain Versailles and return to the National Assembly, where I arrived at ten o'clock. I found no obstacles in my route. About eleven o'clock, several deputies who had left Paris after me came successively to announce to the Assembly that an army of twenty thousand men was marching on Versailles, having at its head M. de La Fayette, that an innumerable troop of women and lowly people formed the advance guard. This news spread consternation in the Assembly, but satisfaction could easily be observed on the faces of the conspirators in it. The deliberations on the agenda continued as if there was nothing to fear, although there were many tumultuous movements in several corners of the hall and in the corridors. At every moment the news was becoming more significant and the danger was increasing. Anxious over the situation of the King, I asked your brother to come with me to find out about it, about four o'clock in the afternoon. We went into the palace and learned that the King was out hunting. We needed to eat a little, not having breakfasted. We went to our apartment, which overlooks the great Royal Court. Scarcely were we served than we saw the King arrive on horseback at a full gallop. We did not take time to finish our frugal meal, but ran to the King's apartment, where all his faithful servitors soon assembled. The apartments were full. All the King's Guards were mounted; there may have been six hundred of them. They lined up in battle formation in the Place d'Armes, the Duke of Guiche at their head. The Swiss Guards joined them. The French Guards had gone to join the insurgents in Paris and to swell the troop which was marching on Versailles. The Flanders regiment was in front of the King's stables; there were also two hundred dragoons of the King's regiment, composing an army of perhaps twenty-four hundred men, who could have been joined by more than four hundred noblemen full of ardor and zeal. We waited to receive the order to march to meet the Parisian column which, I think, would have been easy to disperse. But everyone remained in a state of fatal inaction. The King's Council, divided in opinion, could not decide on any course. The King, in accordance with the advice and urging of MM. de Saint-Priest and La Luzerne, appeared to want to ensure the safety of his person and escape. For this purpose, the King's Guards were ordered over to the garden, where they remained until eleven o'clock in the evening. A carriage had been prepared for the King, and his trunks were being put in, when MM. Necker and de Montmorin came to get these arrangements changed by frightening the King as to the danger of flight.

While the King's Guards were still in battle formation in the Place d'Armes, they were spared no outrages or insults from the National Guard of Versailles and from the people, who had declared themselves in favor of their brothers of Paris. They had likewise corrupted the Flanders regiment, which also went into insurrection. Emissaries of the factious were seen to distribute gold and silver to them. Such was the position of Versailles at six o'clock when the first column of women appeared, led by furious men who incited them as they passed before the hall of the Estates, which is on the main avenue. Most went in there and mixed pell-mell with the deputies. They uttered their threatening vociferations, manifested their bloody projects, including the massacre of the Queen even in the King's arms. The factious in the Assembly were observed to welcome them, mix among them, and encourage them. Several men were clearly seen disguised as women. They asked M. Mounier, president at the time, to come with them in a deputation to the King, on the pretext of asking him for bread. He appeared with twenty of these women at the palace gates; all were closed and guarded. I found myself by chance inside the gate and, recognizing the president, who was being crushed by the crowd, I identified him to the sentinels and the officer of the guard, whom he told of the object of his mission. They let him in with six women, and I accompanied them to the King's apartment, where this deputation was introduced. Among these women I noticed two who appeared quite proper and not at all of the class of people, although affecting their language. They were coming, they said, to ask for bread from the good King. That prince welcomed them and assured them that if it was lacking, this was not his fault. They withdrew, appearing very satisfied to have seen the King. I thought they were even softened by his welcome.

Finally, at eleven o'clock in the evening, the noise of drums announced the arrival of the Parisian army. It had been horrible weather all day, rain and wind, which had slowed its march. At eleven-thirty, the great General La Fayette appeared, covered with mud from head to foot; his soul was still more so, in the eyes of the spectators. He proudly went into the King's cabinet, sought to reassure that prince as to this military visit, said that the Parisians, full of love and respect for His Majesty, did not want to entrust others with guarding his person, that this was the only object of their trip, that everyone could be at ease, that no disorder would be committed, that he had provided for everything. These fine words were repeated to us in the King's chamber, where we were, but we were not reassured by them. It was known that people wanted to attack the King's Guards in the garden where they had been forgotten. They had been ordered to go to Rambouillet, where they went, across the fields, in fear of being pursued.

About an hour after midnight, M. de La Fayette came out of the King's cabinet and said that the King and Queen were going to bed, that he was going to do the same, and that he advised everyone to retire and sleep peacefully, that no one had anything to fear. . . .

Ah, my dear, what a day I have to describe, and what an awakening I had! About six o'clock in the morning, I was awakened by confused noise. I have told you that your brother and I were in the apartment that had been lent to us in his absence by your cousin, the Grand Falconer. It overlooks the Royal Court. At this noise, I jumped from my bed and ran to the window. What a spectacle! I saw the court filled with men and women armed with pikes, sticks, etc., running in every direction like furies, shouting, "No quarter to those beggars, let's go to the Queen's." You can judge of my fright and consternation. I stood still a long time; I saw two different groups dragging two King's Guards toward the gate, where they were massacred; I heard on my stairway the horrible noises of those furious fellows who were going up and down; I really thought it was the last instant of my life. But forgetting myself, I no longer thought of anything but the King's position; I thought of my duty to go and defend his person and die at his feet; I picked up my courage and had myself dressed quickly; your brother was thinking and acting in the same way. While the servant was dressing me, I saw the whole Parisian army enter the court, drums beating, preceded and followed by several cannon, all marching in column. On the flanks were thousands of bandits and women who were running in all directions. The Royal Court and the Marble Court were soon filled by all these people. I found myself puzzled to know how I should be able to reach the King. At all events, I delivered myself over to luck, and having taken my pistols, my sword, and a piece of bread, I went out by a door to the Princes' Court. Your brother went with me, but we were separated by the innumerable crowd of soldiers filling the apartments. I was fortunate, however, to reach the door of the King's chamber. It was closed; I knocked, an usher opened it for me, I told him I was going to find the King, and he let me in. I crossed the Council room, the King's chamber, the Pendulum room, without meeting anyone. Finally I reached a little room where there were a few *valets de chambre*. One of them asked if I wanted to be announced, I said yes, he opened the door of a side room and said I was asking to enter, and I heard the King say, "Yes, yes, let him come in," and I saw that prince before me. He questioned me keenly as to what I had seen. The Queen was so good as to tell me that she believed I would not have been the last to come to them.

I expressed my satisfaction at finding her with the King. She was so good as to recount to me the miraculous manner in which she had reached him with her children. Having heard a great amount of noise in the guard-room and at her door, she had had only enough time to jump from bed, throw on a skirt, and come down by a small hidden staircase into her childern's apartment, from which she took them. She admitted that she thought she was lost when, having climbed up to the little door that leads to the Oeil de Boeuf, through which she wanted to reach the King's apartment, she found it closed from the inside. It was at the moment when the King's Guards who had taken refuge in the Oeil de Boeuf had barricaded themselves in there and were resisting the grenadiers of the French Guards, who wanted to force their way in. She knocked again, louder, and finally they came to open this little door for her, after they heard her voice.

When I was crossing the Oeil de Boeuf to go to the King, I found the King's Guards there mingled with the French Guards and, having made their peace, they were exchanging their shoulder belts and their hats for the grenadiers' caps.

In the inner cabinet room where I found the King, there were only the King, the Queen, the little Dauphin, Madame Royale, Madame de Touzel, the children's governess, Mesdames de Makau and de Soucis, assistant governesses, and the Duke of Liancourt. Your brother arrived almost as soon as I did, in the same way. A quarter of an hour afterward came Monsieur and Madame, the King's aunts, and Madame Elisabeth, who threw herself into her brother's arms, all in tears. Everyone had an air of consternation; only the Queen showed great courage and a good countenance. Successively, many people came, keeping a mournful silence. The ministers came a full half-hour later. M. Necker alone was noticeable for his fine embroidered suit; all the rest of the company was in frock coat. The ministers withdrew with the King into another room.

All the women from Paris had crowded into the Marble Court, their faces turned toward the large balcony. Behind them were all the troops. There arose a general shout, "The King on the balcony," which went on for more than a quarter of an hour. At this moment, M. de La Fayette appeared in the place where we were, all very uneasy over the noise. The Queen took M. de La Fayette to the room were the King had withdrawn with his ministers. A moment later, I saw the King and the Queen go forward onto the balcony. The Queen held the little Dauphin in her arms and her daughter by the hand. I followed immediately after that princess. As soon as the King and the Queen appeared on the balcony, loud shouts of "Vive le Roi!" were heard. M. de La Fayette, who stood between the King and the Queen, signaled with his hat that he wanted to speak and obtained silence. He reminded all those people of the oath and promise he had made for them, to remain faithful to the King and not to commit any disorder; he summoned them to renew the same oath before His Majesty. At once all the people raised their hands, shouting, "Yes, yes, we swear it," and on all sides they repeated the shouts of "Vive le Roi! Vive la Reine!" Then the King asked M. de La Fayette to speak in behalf of the King's Guards. M. de La Fayette again asked for silence and said, "Citizens, you have made a mistake concerning the King's Guards. I am certain that like you they are good citizens, and the King requests you to look upon them and treat them like your brothers." "Yes, yes," shouted everyone on all sides. Then several King's Guards and former grenadiers of the French Guards were brought onto the balcony. They embraced each other fraternally and exchanged hats for grenadiers' caps. They took off their shoulder belts, which they threw to the people, who accepted them with joy. M. de La Fayette again obtained the opportunity to speak; he requested the people to return to Paris, to take the good news of peace, and he made a sign to them to withdraw, but no one moved. The King and the Queen, after having saluted the people, left the balcony with the same acclamations, but a moment later many voices shouted several times, "The Queen on the balcony, alone, alone!" I admit that I could not help feeling terror for that princess. She had the courage to leave her son, whom she still held in her arms, putting him into the hands of the governess; then she appeared alone on the balcony, with an assured countenance, and saluted everyone. Some are sure they heard voices shout, "Shoot, shoot!" but whether her august air impressed the people, repeated shouts of "Vive la Reine" came to our ears and reassured us. She remained for about two minutes in cruel perplexity there. When she had come back into the chamber, she did not conceal the fright she had had; she drew a long sigh and, taking the little Dauphin into her arms again, she covered him with kisses and tears, which made all of us weep. Then she went back with the King into the inner cabinet room, where I followed them. We were hoping that the danger had passed and that at the voice of M. de La Fayette all those people were going to return to Paris, when a half-hour later, numerous shouts were heard: "The King to Paris! The King to Paris! The King on the balcony!" Then there was general consternation inside; every face appeared convulsed. We were throwing ourselves into one another's arms and dissolving in tears. The shouts of the populace redoubled. The King held council for another moment with his ministers. Then he came onto the balcony again, preceded by M. de La Fayette and followed by the Queen, who said, passing in front of me, "We are going to Paris." For a reply, I raised my eyes to Heaven.

M. de La Fayette made a sign asking for silence and said that the King, desiring to satisfy the wishes of the people, had charged him to announce that he had just given orders to prepare his carriages and that he would leave with his family about noon to go to Paris, where he planned to fix his residence. The King also said a few words that I could not hear but which confirmed what M. de La Fayette had just said. You can picture the people's transports of joy. The shouts of "Vive le Roi" were heard several times. As soon as the King had come back into his apartments, all the soldiers fired their muskets and the cannoneers the cannon, which made a terrible noise that frightened all of Versailles for some moments. . . .

Testimony in Paris

The provisional municipal government of Paris created a committee on October 21 to investigate conspiracies intended to foment insurrection. This committee extended its investigations to include the recent events at Versailles. In November, it filed a formal complaint in the Châtelet concerning the "execrable crime" committed in Versailles on October 6 by "bandits, impelled by clandestine maneuvers, who mingled with the citizens." Two judges and a court clerk investigated the complaint, hearing 388 witnesses between December, 1789, and July, 1790, and other judges, in Langres, Pont-Audemer, Annonay, Millau, Geneva, and Limoges, were commissioned to hear eight other witnesses, bringing the total number to 396, whose depositions fill more than 550 closely printed pages.

Important though this material is, as historical evidence it presents particular difficulties originating in the judges' procedure and choice of witnesses. The record of each deposition notes that the deponent swore to tell the truth, that he had been ordered to appear, and that the prosecutor's complaint was read to him; at the end, it notes that the deposition was read back and certified. The reported depositions are not verbatim; most important, they omit the judges' questions, which certainly suggested a number of the witnesses' statements. Much hearsay and faulty recollection is included that would have been examined in a trial, which was never held. About a hundred deponents said they knew nothing about the events. More than sixty deputies in the National Assembly gave depositions, chiefly concerned with the implications for factional politics, which were inconclusive or tendentious. Only twenty-five women living in Paris, and very few from the sections where the women's march began, were called upon to give depositions. The historian's harvest, in short, includes more chaff than wheat.

Excerpts from five depositions are translated here, from *Procédure criminelle instruite au Châtelet de Paris sur la dénonciation des faits arrivés à Versailles dans la journée du 6 octobre 1789* (Paris, 1790), Depositions 35, 82, 105, 187, 343.

December 24, 1789

Maître Gérard-Henri de Blois, age 42, advocate practicing before the Parlement, residing on Rue du Battoir [the westward continuation of Rue Serpente, from Rue Hautefeuille to Rue de l'Éperon]; upon oath . . .

Deposes that as an elected member of the commune he spent the night on duty in the city hall from Sunday to Monday, October 4-5 last. About seven o'clock in the morning Monday he was alone in the police committee room. The first indication of the uprising was the arrest of a baker near Saint-Eustache, accused of having sold a two-pound loaf seven ounces underweight. A detachment of the National Guard brought him in. M. de Gouvion, major-general [of the National Guard], came to notify the deponent, telling him that the people were demanding that this baker be hanged from a lamppost. The deponent, after interrogating the said baker, who admitted his mistake, answered M. de Gouvion, who was fearful that the people might come to take the baker, that they should both do everything they could to prevent such an assassination. This baker, whom the deponent had had hidden, was fortunate enough to escape during the course of the outbreak that began a few moments afterward. About eight o'clock in the morning, informed by M. de Gouvion that the outbreak was definite, that the people were beginning to arrive in the Place de Grève, the deponent in fact saw coming into the court of the city hall a first group of women, most of whom were young, wearing white, their hair dressed and powdered, apparently engaged in a lark and giving no sign of bad intentions. They went up into the various rooms and particularly into the room where the police committee met and into another, next to it, where passports were given out. The deponent conversed with them. They were very polite, [and] he answered all their questions, which had no object other than to learn the purposes of the rooms. A few even asked the deponent to admit a number of women, whom they had forced to follow them, because some were pregnant and others felt indisposed. The deponent had these ladies come in and sit down, offering them aid if they needed any. The number of women increased considerably until about eleven o'clock in the morning. He saw some climb the staircase that leads to the belfry, where they rang the alarm bell. Others laughed, sang, and danced in the court, asking occasionally, "Where is M. Bailly, where is M. de La Fayette?" He also saw women force the jailer to free the detained persons. The deponent noticed two boys, fourteen to fifteen years old, whom he had had taken to the jail that night for having been stopped at an unduly late hour with swordblades concealed in their suits. The deponent remarks that having examined the clothing, figures, and faces of all these women, he noticed very few of them who could be put in the class of vile populace. Having expressed to a few persons his surprise that only the women were coming into the city hall while the Place de Grève was full of men and no one was opposing their entry, he was told that the women had forbidden them to enter. About eleven-thirty, the deponent heard a loud noise from the Arcade Saint-Jean. Having gone over to that side, he saw a considerable number of men force the doors which are under that arcade with big pieces of wood, hammers, and other implements. Soon the doors were broken open, and then a very numerous populace spread to all parts of the city hall, even without coming in by the great staircase at that instant. Seeing all these men and not doubting that they had dangerous projects, the deponent left the city hall, because there were few representatives to the commune and the chiefs of the municipality were not there.

The deponent returned there about two o'clock with M. de Vauvilliers, whom he had encountered in his district, the Cordeliers'. Both went into the police committee room. There the deponent saw the marquis de La Fayette with two grenadiers, formerly in the French Guards, one of whom seemed very heated and was saying to M. de La Fayette, "Mon général, you are being deceived." The latter asked them to indicate the persons who could be abusing his confidence. The grenadier answered, "We will name them to you, but it is necessary to go to Versailles." At these words, M. de La Fayette moved away, still accompanied by the two grenadiers. The deponent could then hear only imperfectly what was said, but an instant later, someone whose name he does not remember told him the grenadiers were forcing M. de La Fayette to go to Versailles; he was opposed to it, pointing out to them that the King could leave his ordinary residence. One of the grenadiers answered, "If the King leaves Versailles, we'll put his son on the throne." This same statement was certainly heard by other persons, since the deponent heard it repeated in the hall of the representatives to the commune, among others by M. Brousse des Faucherets [the vice-mayor]. In the afternoon, when all the representatives to the commune were gathered in the great hall, the deponent saw arriving successively several aides-de-camp of M. de La Fayette to announce that his life was in danger, that he was threatened with being hanged from a lamppost. From all sides were heard shouts, "To Versailles! To Versailles!" Then the assembly thought it was obliged to yield to force and give the order to the general to leave for Versailles. The deponent knows what happened at Versailles only from the public reports.

The deponent adds that he heard members of the police committee say that on Thursday, October 1, there arrived from Holland a sum of six or seven million [livres] which were intended to pay the people to instigate an uprising and to pay the Flanders regiment, which was then in Versailles. As early as Friday and Saturday [October 2 and 3] he was told that the grenadiers of the French Guards had been to Versailles to corrupt the soldiers of the Flanders regiment and take them into the cafés and other public places where they paid considerable expenses for them. Which is all that the deponent said he knows . . . and he signed. . . .

March 5, 1790

Jeanne Martin, age 49, practical nurse, wife of Jean Lavarenne, porter in the d'Aligre town-house, with whom she resides, Rue Bailleul, parish of Saint-Germain-l'Auxerrois; upon oath . . .

Deposes that on Monday, October 5, last, in the morning, in the Louvre Passage near the Infanta garden, she was forced by about forty women to go with them to Versailles; they put a stick in her hand, threatening to mistreat her if she did not march; she remarked to them that she had not had breakfast and did not have a *sou* with her; they answered, "March, march, you won't lack anything." To avoid the ill treatment with which she was threatened, she followed these women; having arrived at the Tuileries and intending to pass through the garden, they encountered the Swiss guard named Frederick who refused to permit it. This gave rise to a brawl between the Swiss and Maillard, who was at their head; the deponent, seeing two swords drawn and fearing a misfortune, struck both swords a blow with the stick she had, which disarmed the combatants; a man armed with a bayonet wanted to fall upon this Swiss; a rather badly dressed woman, holding a rusty sword blade without a hilt, wanted to strike the Swiss a blow; the deponent and other women opposed this, and in the scuffle the deponent was wounded in the hand; they all passed through the Tuileries and continued toward Versailles, with other women who joined them at the Place Louis XV, on the Cours la Reine, and after the city gate; having arrived at Sèvres, near the porcelain factory, they encountered two gentlemen, one wearing a black ribbon, the other dressed in a green suit, who asked them, "Where are you going, ladies?" They replied, "We're going to Versailles, to ask the King for bread for ourselves, our husbands and our children, and for the provisioning of the capital." These individuals said, "Go ahead, behave yourselves, don't be insolent to anyone, and peace be with you." Then a woman whom the deponent does not know but who was armed with a sword said, "Yes, we're going to Versailles; we'll bring back the Queen's head on the end of a sword." The other women made her be silent. The deponent remarks that along the road she saw different couriers pass—among others, one whom the woman wanted to stop and who escaped after having thrown into the river a portfolio he carried; they let pass freely another courier who belonged to the Duke of Orléans and who was leaving Passy to go to Versailles; along the road they saw other couriers.

When they arrived in Versailles, the Flanders regiment was under arms on the left of the palace, and the King's Guards were before the central gate; they presented themselves to enter the court but were prevented from doing so. A man dressed in the uniform of the National Guard of Paris, armed with a saber, crossed the ranks of the King's Guards, one of whom left ranks, ran at him, saber in hand, and hit him a blow which knocked his hat off; three other King's Guards likewise left the ranks, saber in hand, to run after the man in the direction of the barracks; then the deponent lost sight of them. The women, unable to get into the palace court, and the deponent went to the National Assembly; they still had Maillard at their head and about twenty women, of whom the deponent was one. They were brought in to the rail at the front of the National Assembly; they were received with great joy and affability and were seated on a bench; it was Maillard, alone at first, who spoke, asking for bread for them, their husbands, and their children, and the provisioning of the capital. Two members of the Assembly and nine women were appointed as a deputation to the King; only seven went, she was told. The deponent remained at the front rail of the Assembly.

The deputation did not come back from the King until ten o'clock. The King's response was read, then turned over to M. le vicomte de Mirabeau, from whom the deponent received it to turn it over to the said Maillard, who was to bring it back promptly to the city hall. The Assembly having recessed at about one o'clock in the morning, the deponent and many other women slept in the hall. She did not notice any man disguised as a woman, and nothing happened contrary to respectability and decency. At five o'clock in the morning, on Tuesday the 6th, the deponent and two other women whose names and residences she does not know left the hall and went to the Place d'Armes and then to the palace, where she saw the populace arrive in great numbers and climb on the gates in order to get into the palace, which was not opened. At that moment, several King's Guards inside the palace fired musket shots at the people; the deponent noticed and recognized three or four from their uniforms and shoulder belts. This discharge killed a citizen in the Marble Court. The Guard who had killed this citizen was seized by the populace, who took him to the Place d'Armes, where he lost his life. Another King's Guard stabbed a citizen in the arm with a dagger; he was cruelly wounded and carried to the infirmary. This Guard was instantly wounded by a hatchet blow which cut off half his face and then taken to the Place d'Armes, where he was killed beside the first one. A man from the faubourg Saint Antoine who had a long beard and was armed with a hatchet cut the heads off the said King's Guards. Several King's Guards, likewise threatened by the women, were saved by the grenadiers of the National Guard. The deponent helped to parry a lance, which struck her in the right arm and dangerously wounded her.

A short time afterward, M. de La Fayette announced that the King was going to appear; in fact, the King and the royal family appeared on the balcony. Then the people shouted: "Vive le Roi, vive la Nation, vive le Dauphin!" The deponent and a few other women shouted, "Vive la Reine," but women of the common people hit them to make them be quiet. The King and the royal family retired from the balcony. The Queen placed herself at a little window, and while she was there, women of the common people spouted all kinds of insults, which the deponent will not repeat to us here. The people shouted: "Vive le Roi! Le Roi à Paris! Le Roi à Paris!" [The King to Paris!] His Majesty consented to go; more shouts of "Vive le Roi!" were heard. The Queen, accompanied by M. le marquis de La Fayette, appeared on the balcony, and the latter said: "The Queen is distressed at what she sees before her eyes; she has been deceived; she promises that she will be so no longer; she promises to love her people, to be attached to them as Jesus Christ is to His church." As a sign of approval the Queen, tears streaming, raised her hand twice. The King asked for mercy for his Guards, and the people repeated his words. The King's Guards shouted "Vive le Roi! Vive la Nation!" and threw their hats, shoulder belts and, a few, even their money out of the windows. The grenadiers of the National Guard put their caps on the King's Guards' heads and also shouted "Vive le Roi! Vive la Nation!" and at this moment the King declared that at noon he would leave for Paris.

After this, the deponent left, alone, to come back, and along the road, having reached the hamlet at Point-du-Jour, was recognized by persons in a cart who had her get in with them and took her home. The deponent remarks that a few days ago a woman who came to rent in the house where the deponent lives told her that she likewise had been stopped and forced to go to Versailles, that on the road she had requested one of the women to let her go because she had left a small child at home who needed her care, that to obtain her freedom she had suggested that she drink a pint of wine, that they had gone into a cabaret and there she had remarked to the woman that she was barefoot, to which the woman had replied, "It is not for lack of money," and had drawn out of her pocket ten six-franc crowns, all separately wrapped in papers torn from those sheets that are hawked in the streets; which is all the deponent said she knows, . . . and declared that she does not know how to sign . . .

March 19, 1790

Marie-Catherine-Victoire Sacleux, age 31, mistress of a cleaning and dyeing establishment, wife of Jean Nemery, scribe, residing on Rue de la Calandre [a street that was on the Île de la Cité at the location occupied after 1865 by the prefecture of police]; upon oath . . .

Deposes that being unable to obtain bread Saturday, Sunday, and Monday morning, her shop being closed in the public clamor, and having heard that the women were going to the city hall to obtain bread, she went there. She found innumerable women of the common people who, after some talk, said it was necessary to go to Versailles. The deponent, who did not care to go to Versailles, gave as pretexts that she was wearing the wrong shoes for it and that she had to return home. The women opposed this. They even obliged her, with others, to drag one of the three cannon that were at the Place de Grève, which she did, as far as Sèvres; from there, other women dragged the cannon to Versailles.

Having arrived in the Place d'Armes, they encountered King's Guards who opposed their passing. In the scuffle, the deponent was slightly cut on the ring finger of her left hand by either a sword or a saber. A rather well dressed gentleman whom she heard called M. de Guiche asked them what they wanted. Those who were in front said that they were coming to speak to the King and would inform them of his response. The same gentleman took four of them in to M. le comte d'Affry and the latter to M. de Saint-Priest, who brought them in to the King. She knew that the King had said to these women: "Don't worry, in a few days you will have enough to eat."

The deponent and other women appeared at the left wing of the palace to enter it. Swiss guards opposed this. The deponent, indisposed and positively ill, was carried to Rue de Vergennes, to the schoolmaster's, where she remained unconscious a very long time. She was given something that helped her come to, spent the night there, did not go out until about eight o'clock, so that she saw none of what happened at Versailles. In the middle of the morning Tuesday, she saw the King, the Queen, and the royal family on the balcony; in the Marble Court she heard women and National Guardsmen whom she did not observe sufficiently to be able to designate them. She heard some say it was necessary to force a way into the palace in order to compel the King to come to Paris and other soldiers saying it was necessary for the palace to be entered only by women. As eight of the women were preparing to go in, it was announced that the King would come to Paris with the royal family. This announcement was confirmed by His Majesty, who asked for mercy for his guards. At this moment the people shouted, "Mercy for the King's Guards," and the latter threw their hats and shoulder belts out the windows. The King and the royal family having left for Paris, the deponent went home; which is all the deponent said she knows, . . . and she signed . . .

April 23, 1790

Françoise Rolin, age 20, a flowergirl, residing on Rue de la Poterie, at the market, in the house of Plochet, cloth merchant; upon oath . . .

Deposes that on October 5 last, between seven and eight o'clock in the morning, she was leaving her mother's to go out selling when she was stopped by several market women whom she does not know personally, who told her that it was necessary for her to go with them. She asked them where they wanted to go with her. They answered to the city hall, and if they did not obtain satisfaction they would go to Versailles. At the Place de Grève, several of these women went into the city hall and asked for M. Bailly and then M. de La Fayette. They were told that neither was there. Then they left to go to Versailles. It was about noon. Having

reached the main road to Versailles, they encountered about twenty
dragoons, in two groups. The deponent was one of those who asked
them where they were going. They said they were going to Paris
to obtain bread and that at Versailles everyone desired their arrival.

Having arrived at Versailles between four and five o'clock, after a
very heavy rain, they presented themselves at the palace gate and
were refused entry. Several shots were fired; she does not know by
whom. None of the women were wounded, but she saw two horses
that had fallen to the ground. She noticed that those who fired
fled at once. While the other women went to the National Assembly, she and the one called Louison Chabry [a 17-year-old girl who
worked in a woodcarver's shop in Paris] remained in the Place
d'Armes. They spied five men dressed in black coming, followed
by many women who had come with the deponent. She and the
Chabry girl went to meet these gentlemen. The deponent threw
herself at the feet of one of them, telling him that they were un-
done and they desired to go to the King. This gentleman reassured
her, telling her that he was the president of the National Assembly, that he was going with a deputation to the King, and that they
had only to follow him.

Having arrived at the palace gate, the president, whose name,
she knew, was M. Mounier, wanted to have it opened. He was
refused and told that the King was holding council. M. Mounier
said he was surprised at this refusal, because he had always been
free to address the King when he had to speak to him. The comte
d'Estaing arrived at the gate [and] had it opened for the deputies,
remarking that it was not possible for the women to come in with
them, that the King was in council and was already concerned
with securing the bread they were coming to ask for. It was agreed,
however, that four of the women would enter. M. Mounier took
the deponent on his arm, the others went on the arm of other
deputies, and they came into the apartments, to the room where,
she was told, Louis XV's bed is located. Someone came to tell
M. Mounier to come into the room where the King was. The deponent wanted to enter with him but was violently pushed away
by a Swiss guard. She fell to the floor, where she received several
kicks. She was picked up by the comte d'Estaing, who seated her on

a bench; and as she was weeping, the comte d'Estaing said to her, "Are you crying because you have not seen the King?"

[He] then took her by the hand, led her into an apartment in the middle of which there was a large table covered with a green cloth and where there stood the keeper of the seals, a gentleman who, she was told, was M. de Saint-Priest, the duc de Gèvres, and other lords whose names she does not know. There, M. de Saint-Priest asked her what they had come to do. She answered him that she had been forced by several women to come to Versailles. He asked for what reasons. She answered him that they were coming to tell the King that his good city of Paris was lacking bread. M. de Saint-Priest asked her, "Why have you not been to ask for some at the city hall?" She answered, "We have been there, and we found no one." He told her that it was necessary to close the gates and bring the keys away to let the King see that his city was well guarded.

Louison Chabry went out with papers that the King had put in her hands. The deponent went down with her to rejoin the other women who had come from Paris and who had remained outside the palace gate. They showed them what the King had written and told how His Majesty had received them. Those women appeared discontent and supposed that the deponent and Louison Chabry had received money from the King and said that those papers were not signed by him. And although they proved, by turning their pockets inside out, that they did not have a *sou*, those women wanted to hang them, and it was the one named Babet Lairot and Mme. Le Clerc and two King's Guards, one of whom had two crosses, who saved their lives. After this, she and the Chabry girl went back up into the apartments, where the King signed the papers. The comte d'Estaing handed them to a deputy who, followed by the women, carried them to the National Assembly.

While in the hall of the National Assembly, the deponent and other women said that they wanted the King to come to Paris, that he would know better what was happening there and that business would be better. Then one of those gentlemen told them to be quiet, that they did not know what they were asking for. They were offered money, which they refused to accept, saying that they had come only to obtain bread. Then, at ten o'clock, they came back to Paris, in carriages the King had ordered to be provided for them. Having arrived at the city hall, they went inside. The papers were turned over by one of the women. They were given supper, and the deponent got home at five o'clock in the morning. Since then, she has not taken any further steps nor seen anyone. Which is all that she said she knows . . . and declared that she does not know how to sign. . . .

June 18, 1790

Marie-Rose Barré, age 20, unmarried, a lace-worker, residing at 61 Rue Meslay; upon oath . . .

Deposes that on October 5 last, at about eight o'clock in the morning, going to take back some work, she was stopped at the Pont Notre Dame by about a hundred women who told her that it was necessary for her to go with them to Versailles to ask for bread there. Not being able to resist this great number of women, she decided to go with them. At the hamlet at the Point-du-Jour, two young men, unknown to her, who were on foot and going their way, told them that they were running a great risk, that there were cannon mounted at the bridge at Saint Cloud. This did not prevent them from continuing on their way. At Sèvres they had some refreshments; then they continued on their way toward Versailles. The two young men of whom she spoke met them near Viroflay and told them that they had escaped at Saint-Cloud but that at Versailles they would be fired on. But they continued on their way. At Versailles they found the King's Guards lined up in three ranks before the palace. A gentleman dressed in the uniform of the King's Guards, who, she was told, was the duc de Guiche, came to ask them what they wanted of the King, recommending peaceful behavior on their part. They answered that they were coming to ask him for bread. This gentleman was absent for a few minutes and then returned to take four of them to introduce them to the King. The deponent was one of the four. Before taking them to the King, he led them to the comte d'Affry, who requested that they be introduced to His Majesty right away, which was done.

They spoke first to M. de Saint-Priest, and then to His Majesty, whom they asked for bread. His Majesty answered them that he was suffering at least as much as they were, to see them lacking it, and that so far as he was able he had taken care to prevent them from experiencing a dearth. Upon the King's response, they begged him to be so good as to arrange escorts for the flour transports intended for the provisioning of Paris, because according to what they had been told at the bridge in Sèvres by the two young men of whom she spoke earlier, only two wagons out of seventy intended for Paris actually arrived there. The King promised them to have the flour escorted and said that if it depended on him, they would have bread then and there. They took leave of His Majesty and were led, by a gentleman in a blue uniform with red piping, into the apartments and courts of the palace to the ranks of the Flanders regiment, to which they called out, "Vive Le Roi!" It was then about nine o'clock. After this, they retired into a house on Rue Satory and went to bed in a stable. She does not know the names and addresses of the three women introduced to the King with her. Tired from the trip, having a swollen foot, she did not go Tuesday to the palace or the Place d'Armes, knows nothing, as a witness, of what happened there, and came back to Paris between four and five o'clock in the afternoon of that day in a carriage.

She adds that a fortnight later a gentleman whom she heard called M. de Saint-Paul came to her place and asked her to go to a court commissioner to make a formal declaration of what M. de Saint-Priest told her on Monday, October 5, at Versailles, when she presented herself to speak to the King. As the deponent did not know a court commissioner, Saint-Paul suggested Maître Chenu. The deponent remarks that she was then living on Rue du Four at the corner of Rue des Ciseaux. . . . The commissioner . . . took her declaration . . . in which she sets forth that having heard it said, by the two young men mentioned above, that of seventy wagons of flour intended for Paris only two had arrived, she informed M. de Saint-Priest of this, and he answered that as the grain shortage was equally bad everywhere it was not surprising that the inhabitants of places where flour passed through stopped it for their supply. Besides, the threshing season had not yet arrived, which caused the provisions to be smaller than they should be. . . . She told the commissioner that the minister did not say to her what was being attributed to him by the public: "When you had only one king, you had bread; now that you have twelve hundred of them, go and ask them for it," that in fact she did not hear the minister say this. Which is all that the deponent said she knows . . . and she has signed. . . .

Part Three
CHURCH AND STATE

Reforms in the church were very widely urged before the Estates-General met and were made unavoidable by the financial policies adopted by the National Assembly, especially the decision to dispose of church property. The principles, the details, the procedures, and the timing of reform in the church were debated on several occasions and were discussed in a stream of pamphlets during 1790. No single episode can be selected as the decisive turning point, but the state of affairs in November, 1790, illustrates the leading divergent viewpoints.

On July 12, the National Assembly had adopted as part of the new constitution a decree concerning ecclesiastical offices, appointment to benefices, salaries of clergymen, and enforcement of residence by bishops in their dioceses and priests in their parishes: this was the Civil Constitution of the Clergy. (A translation of it has been published by John Hall Stewart, in his *Documentary Survey*.) In November, Pope Pius VI had not yet publicly pronounced upon its acceptability. The archbishops and bishops (there were 136 of them, to be reduced to 83 by the reorganization) did not agree either upon the ultimate acceptability of the legislation or upon what attitude to adopt while awaiting the pope's reaction. The administrative authorities of departments, districts, and municipalities likewise took various tacks, some pressing for immediate enforcement, others delaying more or less overtly.

The Principles of the French Bishops

The archbishop of Aix attempted to unite the French bishops in a policy of patience and at the same time to emphasize to the pope that action by him was needed. He drew up a statement of principles that was approved and signed by twenty-nine other bishops also and printed on November 11; during the ensuing two weeks, it was signed by twenty-five more bishops, and after the committee report of November 26, by over seventy bishops in addition, who thus finally made it overwhelmingly the majority position of the episcopate.

The concluding pages of the statement are translated here, from *Exposition des principes sur la constitution du clergé, par les évêques députés à l'Assemblée Nationale,* pp. 78-94.

The civil power cannot provide an adequate substitute for resignations that have not been submitted, nor for their acceptance; cannot order or forbid delegations of ecclesiastical authority, annul the acts of bishops who want to retain jurisdiction, constrain bishops to usurp a jurisdiction which they believe does not belong to them, or, lastly, refuse the indispensable concourse of the church's authority, without asserting supremacy in purely ecclesiastical matters and over the spiritual jurisdiction of the church; and it is at that point that a schism would commence, a separation of the universal church, another religion to which the National Assembly cannot possibly want to lend its power or subject the nation.

While the error of a moment would draw the civil power beyond its own proper limits, it would not be able to enforce the confidence of the faithful and the obedience of the bishops; it would establish other laws, another discipline, another government which the church does not know; it would follow its principles; and the bishops and the pastors and the faithful would follow those of the church.

It is a purpose of a humane and just government to forbid intolerance and persecution. When legislators have by their decrees protected the freedom of religious opinions, it could not enter their minds to leave all religions free except the one which, still dominant and maintained by the piety of our fathers and by all the laws of the state, has continued for twelve hundred years to be the national religion.

The Protestants are free (is the Catholic religion necessarily to be reduced in France to claiming the rights of another religion?) to mark out as they wish territorial divisions in the exercise of their ministers' functions, and the civil authority does not make laws nor assert the right to constrain them; it cannot exercise, against the ministers of the Catholic religion, a power that it forbids itself to employ towards the ministers of foreign religions; it cannot make it a crime for us to persevere in the principles of the church. It is the faithful themselves whom no authority can turn away from their belief; no one can prohibit them from believing what the church teaches them. Religion is law for those whom it has persuaded; no one can prohibit them from doing in the religious order what religion commands them to do. . . .

If the civil power wants to make changes in the religious order without the concourse of the church, it contradicts principles and does not destroy them; it contradicts principles and destroys the very means which can help to carry out its purposes.

We want to know the wishes of the church, in order to reestablish a necessary agreement between the civil power and the ecclesiastical power and through their union to keep consciences at rest and preserve public tranquillity.

If the church and the state are to cooperate and agree on spiritual objectives and civil purposes, it is necessary that those to whom the divine laws have given the government of the church be able to make themselves heard like those to whom human laws give the government of the state.

The church must be represented, like the nation.

The universal church is represented in ecumenical councils.

The Gallican church is represented in its national councils.

Each church consults, in important cases, the visible head of the universal church; and again we can call for the concourse of the head of the church and of provincial councils.

The express or tacit consent of the universal church, informed in the forms prescribed by constant usage and by the canons, is the true principle of the decisions and laws of the church.

This consent cannot be given in a purely civil assembly; the exercise of the power of the citizens cannot be confused with the expression of the belief of the faithful.

We have proposed the convocation of a national council.

We have called for recourse, according to the ancient forms of the Gallican church, to the head of the universal church.

We have designated the subjects on which the provincial councils would be competent.

We have declared ourselves unable to participate in any deliberations on spiritual subjects by a purely civil power, which cannot be extended to the spiritual jurisdiction of the church.

We have called for recourse to canonical procedures for purely spiritual subjects and for cooperation of the civil power and the ecclesiastical power for mixed subjects.

We have refused to take the oath as to everything that concerns the spiritual subjects depending on the authority of the church.

Finally, we have asked that the National Assembly suspend the decrees' effectiveness in the departments until the church has manifested its wishes by the voice of its visible head or until the canonical procedures have been completed according to the wise and charitable rules that guide the exercise of its power.

There is no legitimate means of examination, of conciliation, and of decision, that we have not proposed, and we shall at least have the advantage of not having neglected anything for the maintenance of principle in a ministry of peace and concord.

Such seemed to be the dispositions of the committee that drew up the decrees; because it recognized the necessity for canonical procedures, it proposed to ask the King to take the necessary measures for carrying them out. . . .

Such were the King's intentions when, ready to give his sanction, he announced that he would take the necessary measures for carrying out the decrees. His Majesty believed himself obliged to inform the head of the church, consult the church, and obtain its response through his voice.

Our request to await his response, in conformity with the bishops' wishes, the rules and customs of the church, the king's intentions, the dispositions with which the decree was proposed, did not contradict any principle, any decree adopted by the National Assembly. . . .

Why has the Assembly itself neither accepted nor rejected the convocation of a national council? . . .

Why has the Assembly not declared the incompetence of the authority that we have called for if the Assembly has no doubt as to its own authority?

The Assembly has feared to compromise the interests of the civil power, by recognizing the boundary between the two powers.

It is because it is aware of the rights of the church that it remains silent. Its silence is an admission of the justice and necessity of our claims. Its conviction, or its doubts, leave standing, with all their strength, the same principles which all the laws have maintained and which make it a duty for us to consult and await the wishes of the church. . . .

When one says that religion depends on the legislators on earth, one assumes that Jesus Christ has not given it his legislators and his guides, one supposes that his legislation does not come from heaven; but we have not made our religion, we have received it from our fathers, as they received it from theirs, going back ultimately to the apostles. Our reason must yield, in order for us to submit to the authority of the earliest times, not only as to dogma, but as to practice.

One cannot believe that religion is the work of God when one wants to subject it to the thoughts of men.

It seems that some persons reason about the discipline of the church as about the regulation of states.

It seems that the people can change the form of their religion like those of their government.

The Christian religion is the law that the father of all men has given them, to guide them on the way to eternity; it must apply to all men; it cannot be true for one people and false for another. . . . It teaches truths of a supernatural order, which have no relation to the administration of empires. It embraces, in its morality, the duties of all states. . . . Political interests and local differences cannot change the principles of a religion whose dogmas are the objects of a supernatural faith and whose morality is universal. The civil laws can cooperate to make public its teaching, to make secure its administration, to make effective the jurisdiction of its ministers; its institutions, which came from Jesus Christ and from the apostles, its divine institutions, which are the principles of the general discipline of the church, cannot be formed by a purely civil legislation.

We want to avoid schism; we want to employ all the means that wisdom and charity can suggest to prevent the troubles which a deplorable scission is capable of producing. We cannot introduce schism into our principles when, in our conduct, we are seeking every means to preserve the nation from it.

We have not only set forth principles; we have considered their relation to the different measures that can result from the various inclinations of religious zeal in difficult circumstances; and we think that our first duty is to await, with confidence, the response of Saint Peter's successor, who, placed at the center of Catholic unity and of the communion, must utter and interpret the wishes of the universal church.

Paris, October 30, 1790.

[Signatures of cardinal de La Rochefoucauld, archbishop of Rouen; Talleyrand-Périgord, archbishop of Reims (uncle of the archbishop of Autun who later became a diplomat and foreign minister); Boisgelin, archbishop of Aix; Dulau, archbishop of Arles; Bernis, coadjutor of Albi (nephew of the cardinal then representing the king at the Vatican); Fontanges, archbishop of Toulouse; Chastenet de Puységur, archbishop of Bourges; and the following bishops: Beaupoil de Saint-Aulaire, of Poitiers; Le Tonnelier de Breteuil, of Montauban; Anterroche, of Condom; Jouffroy de Gonssans, of Le Mans; Cortois de Balore, of Nîmes; Colbert de Castle-Hill, of Rodez; Du Plessis d'Argentré, of Limoges; Malide, of Montpellier; Leyris d'Esponchez, of Perpignan; Usson de Bonnac, of Agen; Lubersac, of Chartres; Sabran, of Laon; Ruffo, of Saint-Flour; Clermont-Tonnerre, of Châlons-sur-Marne; Villoutreix de Faye, of Oléron; Des Monstiers de Mérinville, of Dijon; La Rochefoucauld-Bayers, of Beauvais; La Rochefoucauld-Bayers, of Saintes (brother of the preceding); Talalu de Chalmazel, of Coutances; Mercy, of Luçon; Bonal, of Clermont-Ferrand; Béthisy de Mézières, of Uzès; Lastic, of Couserans.]

The Debate over the Oath of Loyalty

While the thirty bishops were agreeing on their statement, the National Assembly was led to consider ways of exacting obedience to its decree. On November 6, a deputy reported that the cathedral chapter of Cambrai had protested against the effort of local administrators to place its movable property under official seal as national property. Another deputy moved to authorize local administrations to withhold salaries from clergymen who protested against the Assembly's decrees. The proposal was referred to the committee on ecclesiastical affairs, for report. The report, when submitted on November 26, came jointly from four committees: on ecclesiastical affairs, nationalized property, reports, and investigations. It had been prepared principally by the chairman of the committee on investigations, Voidel, a 31-year-old lawyer from Lorraine who was a freemason, a Jacobin, and brother of a parish priest. He recommended a decree requiring bishops and parish priests to be replaced if they refused to take an oath, in public after mass, "to be faithful to the nation, the law, and the King, to maintain with all their power the constitution decreed by the National Assembly and accepted by the King."

The report was the subject of debate during two evening sessions, led off by François de Bonal, bishop of Clermont-Ferrand, with a statement prepared in advance, seemingly as the chosen spokesman for many of the bishops. Voidel's report and de Bonal's statement were both printed as pamphlets within a few days and reprinted later in the *Archives Parlementaires,* Mavidal and Laurent, eds. (Paris, 1867-1913), XXI, 3-10.

Report by Voidel

Gentlemen, religion is the basis of the morality of beneficent and just actions. It offers the virtuous man the deepest consolations in misfortune; it applies to the wicked a redoubtable and salutary restraint; in the former's heart and in the latter's conscience it places its tribunal and holds its sway. The friend of order and society, independent of men, of times and places, eternal as its divine author, it triumphs over all passions, it defeats all prejudices. Superstition and fanaticism can indeed darken, even disfigure it; they cannot change it. I thought myself obliged, gentlemen, thus to begin with this striking and sincere homage to the religion of my fathers, a report in which I shall be forced to inveigh against the crimes of those who teach it, who slander it by their conduct, who cause it to appear hateful in the eyes of superficial or corrupt men who do not know it and who see in it only the misconduct of its ministers.

Consider it in its origin, follow it in its progress, consult it especially in that Book which, well pondered, would alone suffice for the instruction and happiness of men and whose religious and civil maxims you can find analyzed in your declaration of rights, in your constitution, and especially in your decree on the civil organization of the clergy; everywhere it recommends peace, everywhere it preaches respect and submission to laws; that is what belongs to it. . . .

A league has been formed against the State and against religion among a few bishops, a few chapters, and a few parish priests. Religion is its pretext; interest and ambition are its motive. To show the people by a combined resistance that one can with impunity brave the law; to teach them to scorn, train them to revolt, dissolve all the bonds of the social contract; excite war; those are the methods, and the facts prove it. . . .

This plan is to be found outlined in a letter of the former bishop of Tréguier to the parish priests of that diocese. After having declared that he will regard as intruders the bishops and parish priests named in accordance with the new procedures, he vows that he will not communicate with them in divinis. . . .

It contains, finally, this remarkable passage which alone reveals the league's secret: "In all times, but particularly in this, we must be unius labii, and our conduct must be the same; this unity ought to produce the fortunate effect we intend." And so that their conduct will be the same, he sends them a formula of a protest, which several have signed and which excludes not only the absolute law but even the concourse of the sovereign in dividing the dioceses. . . .

The other refractory bishops do not, it is true, express their ideas in such absolute terms; more reserved or more adroit, the bishops of Soissons, Dijon, Verdun, and Nantes limit themselves to protesting the incompetence of the sovereign while declaring that in order to come to a decision they are waiting for the response of the Roman pontiff to the letter that the King, it is said, has written to him.

You will see, gentlemen, that the rebels, though united in resistance, give effect to it differently in accordance with their various passions, their fears, or their expectations. . . .

Thus the bishop of Beauvais, a member of this Assembly, pressed by the directory of the Oise department to give orders in his diocese for promptly carrying out the decree on the civil constitution of the clergy, the conversion of his cathedral into a parish church, the elimination of [superfluous] parishes, the appointment of his vicars, answered that not knowing when your session will end, he was not able to schedule his return. But on October 14 the living of Puisieux, in the district of Senlis, became vacant; on the 22nd the bishop of Beauvais appointed Quignon, who took possession the 27th, following the old procedures.

Thus the bishop of Lisieux protests that until the Roman pontiff's response to the King he will not obey the decree; he says the bond by which he is attached to the people of his diocese cannot be broken except by a canonical judgment or by his resignation, freely given and freely accepted by the pope; your decree of July 12, he says, is irreconcilable with the fundamentals of the divine hierarchy of the Church. . . .

Thus the bishop of Dijon announces that for the time being he intends to exercise his episcopal jurisdiction only over the places subject to it heretofore, reserving the opportunity of stating his opinion anew when informed of the pope's response. . . .

Thus the bishop of Nantes, in a letter dated Paris, October 16, to the directory of the Loire-Inférieure department, after announcing that he has read the notification brought to him the 5th "in his palace," protests against the elimination of the cathedral chapter and the office of canon, against the conversion of his cathedral into a parish church and the addition of several other livings to it; all operations, he says, capable of being done only by the ecclesiastical power and following canonical procedures.

You will have noticed, gentlemen, in the protests I have just reported to you, that nothing of any sort is said about the sale of the national property [former church property], and as it is not possible, after what we have seen and heard, to suspect the bishops of indifference on that subject, we must be grateful to them for this self-restraint.

You will not find it, gentlemen, in the protests by most of the cathedral chapters. . . . [citing those of Lyon, Saint-Brieuc, Vannes, Quimper, Laon].

One hundred and three parish priests and their vicars in the Loire-Inférieure department have likewise protested against the decree of July 12 and against the alleged incompetence of the National Assembly; they ask that the Catholic religion be declared the only State religion. . . .

To these general and combined protests we must add facts which appear to be isolated but which, in their result, further the league's plans . . . [citing actions and statements of a cathedral canon in Tours, a priest in Rouen, parish priests in five scattered villages] . . .

But, gentlemen, having told you of so many disorders, I would be wrong not to say that amid this subversion of religious principles and of social ideas, men are to be found who have known how to resist the solicitations, the intrigues, and inspirations to hatred of their colleagues and of the prelates; priests truly worthy of the name [citing a cathedral canon in Vannes, another in Laon, the parish priest (and mayor) of Chavignon in the diocese of Soissons, the parish priest of Saint-Cyr in Laon, twenty-four members of the cathedral chapter of Saint-Jean in Lyon].

I am also obliged to praise the active zeal, the enlightened patriotism and the wise firmness of the following administrative bodies: the departments of Maine-et-Loire, Rhône-et-Loire, Aisne, Oise, Loire-Inférieure, Côtes-du-Nord, Morbihan, Finistère [the last four all in Brittany]; the districts of Quimperlé, Vienne, Pont-Croix, Pontivy, Nantes, Savenay, Broons, La Tour du Pin and Guingamp; the municipalities of Soissons, Saint-Brieuc, Rouen, Lyon and Quimper.

Investigations, ordinances, addresses, proclamations: they have done everything that could secure the effectiveness of the law; yet they point out the slowness of your justice; they call loudly for the laws' vengeance upon the guilty; they tell you that examples are needed and that if you want to maintain the Constitution, you must enact a severe law to force the factious to order and the rebels to obedience.

Your committees might perhaps have refrained, gentlemen, from examining and discussing the accusations made by the discontented against the constitutional law of July 12. When the public will is expressed, individuals are obliged to obey, but it is still necessary to remove their pretexts; they must no longer be able to say that you have attacked religion, destroyed the Church hierarchy, broken the unity of the episcopate, interrupted the communion with the Roman pontiff; . . . they must not be able to speak further of the necessity for a council, or to censure the refusal to declare the Catholic religion the only State religion, or to cry out against the alleged defectiveness of popular elections. . . .

They say a political law is incapable of moving the boundaries of the dioceses. Well, let us suppose this for a moment; but the bishop of Soissons admits that in case of an absolute necessity he can exercise jurisdiction over a foreign territory. Is it, then, not an absolute necessity to maintain public peace and give the people an example of obedience to the laws? The bishop of Lisieux says no one can perform acts of episcopal jurisdiction in my diocese until after my voluntary resignation. What! Your resignation can restore peace in France, and you are still a bishop? After so many sacrifices offered to ambition, do you not know how to make them to our country? Why do you not imitate the bishop of Saint-Malo? He had the same ideas as you concerning the supremacy of ecclesiastical power; he has not disobeyed; he left, to the regret of his diocesans; he has fulfilled the holiest of his duties. . . .

They also reproach you, gentlemen, for not having declared solemnly, in your decree of April 13, that the Catholic religion is the sole religion of the State. It is true, you did not want to give weapons to fanaticism; you wanted to preserve for all citizens the right they hold from nature: freedom of religious opinions. But you have done much more for the religion of your fathers; you have declared that, for it alone, you would make a public expenditure; you have destroyed the abuses which had previously caused the scission of our unfortunate fellow citizens; you have thus prepared the way for reunion and the reign of a political and religious confraternity which is destined one day to show the world the happy effects of a wise tolerance.

They reproach you, finally, gentlemen, for the defects of popular elections. Well, only one bishop has been elected by the people so far; and if all France had elected the successor to the bishop of Quimper, it would not have been able to name one who would have been preferable to the abbé Expilly [rector of the parish of Saint-Martin in Morlaix, deputy in the Assembly for the clergy of the diocese of Saint-Pol-de-Léon].

Speaking of popular choices! You are not speaking of those which used to be made by ministers, clerks, valets, women— Excuse me, I have already said more than enough.

Ministers of religion! Stop wrapping yourselves in pretexts; admit your weakness: you regret losing your former opulence; you regret losing those prerogatives, those marks of distinction and of alleged preeminence, all those crutches for vanity which were degrading the house of the Lord. . . . By the force of your virtues, enforce respect from us; you no longer have any means but this to obtain it. Forget your ancient errors, renounce your prejudices, no longer think of those properties you lost; they are going to be sold; for, despite all your efforts, the nation knows that it has the national confidence; that the guarantee of a great people is surer than your predictions; it will not forget that its representatives' first act in its name was to ensure the firmness of its financial obligations.

There is still time; by a prompt submission, disarm the people, angered by your resistance. The decree that I am going to present is not so much a severe law as a measure of indulgence. [Reading of the decree proposed, requiring an oath whose wording has been given above, p. 74.]

Statement by the Bishop of Clermont-Ferrand

Gentlemen, it is not to repel the sarcasms in which the committee spokesman has indulged at the expense of the clergy; it is not to combat his reasonings, which sound logic disavows; it is not to defend the salaries that he proposes to have you take from us; it is not to complain or grumble over the rigor of the decree with which we are threatened, that I have asked to speak.

Strengthened by God's grace against trials of every kind, we hope that our conduct will always show only patience and resignation with firmness. These virtues, which we are obligated to exemplify, are the fruits of the faith we have been called to preach, are charged to defend, and are obliged to heed in all its dictates.

Great interests, gentlemen, absorb lesser ones and cause them to be forgotten. Here we leave all things temporal; neither our position nor our sentiments concern them when what is involved is much more essential to the Church: the hierarchy, jurisdiction, and discipline.

As far from enthusiasm and fanaticism as from the spirit of faction and trouble, dominated by the sole ambition to fulfill our duties and satisfy our conscience, we have again looked into, on the one hand, the sacred books that contain the great principles which must direct us; on the other, the constitution of the clergy.

In that constitution, which you call civil and which, therefore, should treat only civil and political subjects, we could not fail to recognize legislation on spiritual subjects. Grant jurisdiction, withdraw it, extend it or limit it, regulate its exercise, determine its functions, that is what this legislation does; but that is also what the holy books and tradition, venerable and constant, the chain whose first link is fastened to the angular rock on which the Church is built, tell us legislation cannot do; that is what we shall never be able to regard as compatible with the principles of the Catholic Church.

You respect that Church, gentlemen, and you glory in being its children; we like to believe that it is even from zeal for it that several of you have adopted, in great part, the proposed constitutional articles, as supposing they will restore the brilliance of its original beauty. But we are obliged to say—because we cannot keep the truth captive in us, and to utter it freely in your presence is to render homage to you—that the Son of God did not leave his work imperfect when he formed his Church; he organized it himself and left to his apostles the power, which was to be transmitted to their successors, to govern it—the power of making laws, of regulating the functions of the different classes of ministers, of assigning to each one the sphere within which he would be able to exercise his jurisdiction, of perpetuating themselves through ordination, of establishing the canonical order to fill the different places in the sanctuary. Every other organization is foreign to the Church and can have no place in it but by its adoption.

Deign to permit us to assemble in council [loud objections from deputies, reported by the newspaper *Moniteur*]; there, still at one with Peter's successor, we shall seek, in all the purity of purpose to which we are obligated, to reconcile, as far as it is in us, the interests of the nation with those of the holy religion that we must all regard as the most precious national property. Wait, at least, as we have asked several times, for the head of the Church, consulted by the King, to declare himself.

Gentlemen, nothing can better prove to you, as well as to the nation and to the entire world, that we are guided by motives worthy of our places than our resolution, which is necessarily unshakable because it is determined by the most sacred duties, to subject ourselves to every privation and to yield to every sacrifice rather than depart from our principles and betray our conscience.

Thereby, we will provide for our detractors and our enemies, for the foolish as for the wise, for the weak as for the powerful, the fine spectacle that the Church has commanded us to provide when it is a matter of the interests of God. If we have to suffer, we glory in suffering for his cause; we rejoice to become more like his divine son; we abandon ourselves to his providence; our privations will be our pleasures, and the world will know that it is not love of earthly goods which rules our hearts.

For the rest, gentlemen, we repeat, and we are glad to repeat, that in everything civil and political, no submission will exceed ours; we shall not cease to show, by our conduct, as we have several times here solemnly expressed, our fidelity to the law, to the nation and to the King; our ministry will always be devoted, as it must be, to securing and strengthening peace, order, obedience to legitimate authority, of which the Catholic religion is the firmest support, and our hearts will always be active in forming desires for the public happiness.

I beg the Assembly to order that what I have just said be inserted in its minutes of proceedings.

[The bishops and the greater number of the clergy rose as a sign of agreement at the moment when de Bonal left the platform, according to the pamphlet publication of his statement. The majority of the Assembly objected, according to the *Moniteur*.]

The Opinion of a Gallican Lawyer

After the statement by the bishop of Clermont-Ferrand, there were demagogic speeches by Mirabeau, who urged sterner action against recalcitrant clergymen, and abbé Maury, who ridiculed Mirabeau's ignorance of theology and moved postponement of any action; Pétion contributed a phrase ("Theology is to religion what chicanery is to justice") and general support for Mirabeau's proposals. The decisive speech came on the second day of debate, from Armand-Gaston Camus, a lawyer, counsel to the Clergy of France as a corporate body, and a devout believer, of a Jansenist persuasion. He argued against delay in adopting the decree proposed by Voidel, saying it was necessary to put an end to civil disobedience by making clear that violations of the law would be punished. He then went on to discuss the Assembly's authority to enact the constitution of the clergy and the question of papal sanction; these parts of his speech, slightly modified, were printed in a pamphlet in December with an added section answering the bishops' principles. The pamphlet version was signed, to indicate agreement, by 27 deputies who were parish priests; 24 of these, together with 38 other deputies who were priests, took the required oath on December 27, while the majority of clerical deputies sat in silent refusal.

The pamphlet version of the opinion of Camus was reprinted in *Archives Parlementaires*, XXI, 95-103.

The National Assembly's attention was fixed on three points: (1) the authority of the nation, represented by the Assembly, to enact the laws that exist today on the constitution of the clergy; (2) whether or not to delay carrying out those laws, to await the pope's decision; (3) the accuracy or inaccuracy of the principles set forth by the bishops in their statement of October 30. It is on these three subjects that I shall explain my opinion, successively.

1. The nation assembled through its representatives established, on the unchangeable basis of the rights of man, the French Constitution. It distributed the powers necessary to maintain order; it examined all the arrangements which together tend to the people's happiness; it was obliged to examine the state of religion, of its observances, of its ministers; it determined them. . . .

The nation's Assembly, when it was deliberating on religion, incontestably had the right to declare what religion it would maintain. It would have committed an unfortunate and condemnable abuse of its power if it had preferred any but the true religion, the Catholic religion. And so the Assembly did not even think it necessary to deliberate on that subject. It deliberated only in order to decree that there would be bishops in the departments, priests in the parishes; that the observances in conformity with the Catholic religion would be supported by State expenditures; even that these observances would be the only ones paid for by the State. As to the rest, general assent appeared preferable to any deliberation. It is far from being the case, then, that it ever entered the National Assembly's mind to reject the Catholic religion; but what it did not do, it had the power to do; a wretched power, a melancholy power, merely to be guilty, but a power which was no less real in the Assembly and the nation.

In freely maintaining the Catholic religion in the kingdom, at the moment when France is providing itself a new Constitution, the National Assembly was exactly in the position of a State into which Catholic missionaries come and ask to be received. It is a generally known axiom that religion is in the State and not the State in the religion—consequently that the religion must be received in the State, must be knowingly admitted, and that everything that is only a matter of discipline is subject to the modifications required by the State, which, in receiving the religion, dictates to its ministers the conditions under which it consents to receive them. . . .

Now, who would dare to deny that when the Christian religion is received in a State, that State has the right to assign both the number and the locations of the parishes, bishoprics, and metropolitan sees? What missionary worthy of his vocation would refuse to preach the Gospel because, when he announces that it is essential to the Christian religion to have bishops and parish priests, the nation declares to him that it will consent to the establishment of ten bishoprics rather than twenty; of a thousand parishes rather than twelve hundred? The necessity to have bishops and parish priests is a matter of the Catholic faith. It is not a matter of faith that in the space of a hundred leagues, there must be one or two bishops, a hundred or a hundred and fifty parish priests. These external arrangements are to be supplied by the will of a nation which exercises its sovereignty in receiving the Christian religion or in maintaining it. If the Church has some power in this regard, it is only the power to do everything appropriate to conform to the will of the sovereign and to carry it out. . . .

[Narration of the arrival and acceptance of missionaries in England, in 597, to show that ecclesiastical history confirms the preceding paragraph.]

It has been objected that the effect of the Assembly's decrees is to suppress bishoprics and parishes without any formality, a thing absolutely new and contrary to the canons of the councils.

This objection is a sophism which comes from confusing the different kinds of laws that regulate the actions of men. Montesquieu, with great good sense, said: "There are different orders of laws; and human reason is sublime in that it can know to which of these orders the things to be decided are principally related, and not confuse the principles that are to govern men." (*The Spirit of the Laws,* book xxvi, chapter 1.) When a people has a fixed Constitution, or lives as if it had a Constitution, when there are laws enacted to regulate the different acts of civil life and courts to apply them, then these courts, before which individuals appear to defend their interests, ought not to examine whether the Constitution exists or does not exist or whether the existing laws are the best possible laws. Such as the laws are, the courts must apply them; and supposing that the Constitution is null or defective, the laws feeble and insufficient for the people's happiness, still men are happy, in a state so miserable, to have some authority to call upon that sometimes protects them from the caprices of the great or the enterprises of the wicked. . . .

This was the position of France, and—to keep to the subject that is involved here, the suppression of ecclesiastical benefices—the considerable changes that morals, usages, local circumstances had introduced, made it useful frequently to suppress benefices, to unite them to others, to apply their revenues to new purposes. But these operations were turned over to individuals capable of abusing their power. It was necessary to counterbalance the excess of that power and to prevent its abuse by long and difficult procedures. Experience had, more than once, brought an awareness of the disadvantages of these procedures; there had been efforts to abolish them, but there had always been reluctance from fear of rendering unions and suppressions arbitrary; the procedures were retained as the only safeguards against oppression. It was, then, the duty of the jurists and canonists, when they received denunciations of suppressions or unions of benefices decided on by the despotism of the King's agents or the despotism of the bishops, to search in the existing laws, in those voluminous collections of conciliar decrees, royal laws, even judicial decisions, in the authorities capable of supporting good law, for some means to stop arbitrary power; such was the existing order of things.

It would be delirium to claim to carry on these procedures and this plan of conduct in an order of things absolutely different; to try to stop a nation by procedures, a legislator by judicial decisions; to prevent a people from ordering its Constitution, because there exist particular decisions handed down with other purposes in view. Have they forgotten what sovereignty is? Do they still not recognize that sovereignty can belong only to the peoples or to their representatives, never to their agents? . . . It is absurd to say to the French people: "You are regulating the number of bishoprics without taking the advice of the pope, you are suppressing parishes without following procedure, and you are joining benefices together without letters patent registered in the court records."

The futility of such objections strikes every impartial and sensible person. The power of the nation to control, without altering dogma in any way, that which has to do only with the externals of the religion it receives or maintains in the State, is indubitable. . . .

The objection that the nation lacked power having been disposed of, there is another objection that was made to its representatives. Why, it has been said, refuse to have some consideration for souls perhaps too easily alarmed, who beg you to let their scruples be met by the authority of a decision emanating from the pope. This decision has been asked for; it is expected soon; it is expected to be favorable; and, in the minds of those who desire it, as the pope exercises the whole authority of the Church when circumstances do not permit it to assemble, a word on his part will eliminate all difficulties, will calm all anxieties.

What! The French nation has broken the chains that were holding it captive in its own land only to submit to a foreign power? It has raised its head above those of the other peoples only to bow it before the bishop of Rome? And its Church, which gloried in having constantly defended its liberty against ultramontane enterprises, is to lose that precious liberty, preserved by such long and generous efforts, at the moment when the nation is acquiring its liberty!

What is the pope? A bishop, a minister of Jesus Christ like all the other bishops, established to teach the peoples and administer the sacraments, like all the other bishops; whose ordinary functions are limited to the diocese of Rome in the same way that the functions of the other bishops are limited to their dioceses.

The pope has also the character of a metropolitan, and in that character, like every metropolitan, he has the right to provide against negligence on the part of his suffragan bishops who form what is called the province of Rome.

Besides these two titles of bishop and metropolitan, the pope has a special title, which is that of center of unity. He has that character because he is seated on the chair of Saint Peter, of the first of the apostles. . . .

The primacy of Saint Peter did not destroy the mission and the power of the other apostles . . . [citations of the New Testament.]

Persons who are not accustomed to go back to the sources and who believe that what is true and good is only what they have seen done, without knowing why it is done, will be surprised at these truths. They have seen the pope grant dispensations, issue bulls to nominate bishops, to displace or join bishoprics; they have concluded from this that the pope had the right to do all that they have seen him do; and today they are being made to fear that it is to attack religion, the Catholic faith, to take from the pope what they regard as rights that belong to him.

But these persons, if they are of right and impartial mind, will soon be led back to the truth. From their little information about the rules of the Catholic faith, they ought to know that what belongs to faith is only that which has been believed at all times and by all the faithful. This rule applies to the primacy of the pope, to his jurisdiction and his authority to inspect; he has always been regarded as having these rights in all the places where people profess the Catholic faith; but it is far from true that it is the same for the other rights that some would now like to preserve for him. There is not one of them for which we do not know the origin and for which we are not able to indicate the date of origin, very much later than the establishment of the Christian faith.

Ecclesiastical history shows us how the popes, consulted at first voluntarily because of the respect inspired by the first see and the virtues of those who were seated on it, tried to change their advice into decisions; how, on the pretext of coming to the assistance of the oppressed, they attributed to themselves a right to revise the judgment pronounced in the provinces. We can see in that history the firm resistance of the bishops of Africa to this usurpation; but soon the church of Africa perished amid the ravages of wars; the Greek church, separating from Rome, delivered the bishops of Rome from adversaries who had their eyes attentively fixed on his enterprises; in the Latin church it was gradually tolerated that the pope extend beyond Italy the legitimate rights he was exercising in his metropolitan jurisdiction. . . . [The false decretals; the schism of Avignon; the conciliar movement; the concordat of Bologna of 1516.]

Whatever the causes of the aggrandisement of the pope's power, whether their ambition and their policy, the bishops' ignorance or their soft compliance, or the princes' unconcern or their personal interests, it is certain that none of these causes was capable of injuring the imprescriptible rights of the people; and one of these rights is incontestably that which belongs to every society, to live independent of any foreign authority whatever; to require ministers and agents, whom it supports for public order, to perform entirely the functions of their office without obliging the people to send afar for the assistance and the decisions that they ought to obtain in the same places where these ministers and agents are established. The bishops, not being instituted by themselves but by the people for the people, it belongs to the latter to require the bishops to perform all the functions of their ministry.

. . . We have the power to make good laws on all the matters which interest the nation and yet we are not able to fix the number of our bishops without waiting for the pope's sanction. What is this new kind of veto, which comes to us from beyond the mountains and which for so many reasons may have a dangerous influence!

The consequence of these reflections is that the National Assembly has done all that it was obliged to in declaring expressly that it will preserve forever the unity of communion with Saint Peter's successor, visible head of the Church; that there is no need for the pope's sanction and his consent to legitimize and execute the operations that it has decreed relative to the arrangement of the bishoprics; that it would be infinitely dangerous for the Assembly to solicit the pope's consent or recognize either its necessity or its utility, because this would do a mortal injury to the liberty of the Gallican Church.

3. It remains to propose, as I have promised, a few reflections on the *Exposition des principes sur la constitution du clergé*. They will be summary: the circumstances require it, and the order of the *Exposition* makes it easy to combat in a few words.

I was struck first by the very title of the *Exposition*. It is written by bishops who are deputies to the National Assembly; it is signed by thirty bishops and is signed only by bishops. On other occasions, the bishops have added to their signature those of a few of the parish priests who were of their opinion. Why have they not admitted them in the present circumstances? Is this a remnant of those ambitious ideas that the bishops announced at other times, that, as soon as the faith is involved, they alone are the judges and that the priests, although clothed in the same sacerdotal character, ought not to express their sentiments in a dogmatic manner? . . .

Is still another commentary needed on the well-known text of Saint Jerome, *Quid facit, excepta ordinatione, episcopus quod non faciat presbyter?* What does the bishop do, except confer the ministry by ordination, that the priest does not do?

. . . It is reprehensible . . . the repeated outcry that, despite the Assembly's decrees, the Church will preserve its doctrine; that the civil power vainly wants to make changes "in the religious order"; that "there is only one religion" and "political interests and local differences cannot change the principles of a religion whose dogmas are the objects of a supernatural faith." Let the bishops say, then, what is the dogma, the object of a supernatural faith, that a nation contradicts and combats when, in fixing its Constitution and having divided its territory into eighty-three departments, it declares that it wants only one bishop for each department?

The peoples are being alarmed over the Assembly's respect for the dogmas of the Catholic faith. These alarms are vain; this has been proved; the faith will remain whole in France whether there are eighteen archbishoprics and a hundred eighteen bishoprics or only eighty-three bishoprics of which ten are metropolitan. . . . [Citations of the New Testament.]

The election of the parish priests has been turned over to the people. Elsewhere examples of that discipline have been cited, and how is it contrary to the spirit of the apostles? . . .

The right to approve, as preachers or confessors, priests who have already received by ordination the power to preach and hear confessions is said to have been attached at all times to episcopal jurisdiction. How can anyone, no matter how little informed concerning ecclesiastical discipline, be persuaded of such a proposition? The persons who have done the most acccurate research on this matter have found no vestiges of episcopal approbation given to a priest before the fourteenth or fifteenth century; and, in fact, the bishops do not cite in proof of their assertion any texts other than those of the Council of Trent, in the middle of the sixteenth century. . . .

Let us not look in old laws for a new discipline. The truth is that the necessity of episcopal approbation was introduced by the Council of Trent; that that council's decrees not being received in France, the bishops were not able, in virtue of its decree, to subject priests to the law of approbation. It was only in 1695 that the necessity of approbation for every priest appointed to a benefice without pastoral duties became a law by Articles 10 and 11 of the edict of April, 1695. Now we ask of every just and impartial mind: If Louis XIV was able by an edict to subject priests to the necessity of episcopal approbation, how is it that the National Assembly does not have the power to abrogate that law?

Let us therefore repeat confidently, these are vain terrors that the bishops seek to excite in the people's mind. And what is the purpose of these terrors? It is to divert them from the obedience they owe to the laws of the kingdom, to the decrees of the National Assembly accepted by the King.

Since the people's pastors force on them the necessity of examining the principles of their conduct and of making a distinction between those who are preaching contradictory truths, let the people open the Gospel, and let them read there what fruits the doctrine being taught them must bear, which will assure them of the truth of that doctrine. One of the most precious fruits that religion can bear is peace among men, unity, charity. Charity, the virtue whose rules are superior to all others, excuses us from all others, is not itself susceptible of any dispensation. Have the authors of the *Exposition* not pronounced judgment on themselves when they say that "the bishops must be ready to stand aside to avoid schism and maintain unity?" They say they fear the danger of schism; they foretell it, and they remain bishops! They fear that they will be called deserters of their churches, but it is not deserting one's church to give it peace. Desertion is a crime; renunciation of functions that one can no longer usefully perform is a duty. Let the conduct of the bishops show them to us suffused with charity for the souls confided to their care; let them secure peace for us, or let them admit being unworthy to keep the name of pastors.

Part Four

🕮 THE CAPTURE OF THE
TUILERIES PALACE, 1792

The National Constituent Assembly succeeded in establishing in Paris a new municipal government. Its basis was the subdivision of the city into 48 sections, each serving as an electoral district and as the jurisdiction of a battalion of the National Guard. But the Assembly was unable to develop a practicable division of authority between the King, his ministers, and itself. This problem was greatly aggravated by the King's effort to flee the country, in June, 1791, which ended in his capture at Varennes; and it was further complicated by the prospect of Prussian and Austrian intervention, threatened in a declaration of the two rulers issued from Pillnitz. The unsolved problem at the center of government was bequeathed to the new National Legislative Assembly, which sat for one year beginning in September, 1791. The King was advised to rely on armed assistance from Prussian and Austrian troops who could be brought into France by means of a war. Leading members of the Legislative Assembly came to believe that war would force the King to choose between cooperating with the Assembly and revealing himself as a traitor.

In March, 1792, the King was induced to appoint as ministers Roland and Clavière, who were friends of Brissot and other leading legislators. The most important minister, however, was General Dumouriez, who favored war as much as the majority of the Assembly but with the objective of strengthening the royal ministry, not making it dependent on the legislators. War was declared in April, and went badly for the French.

At the end of May, the Assembly adopted a decree requiring the deportation of priests who had not taken the oath to the constitution. The King was unwilling to sanction it. The Assembly voted to abolish the royal guard, to which the King agreed; but many of the guardsmen remained in Paris. Then, on June 7, the Assembly adopted a measure calling for 20,000 volunteers from all over the country (hence their denomination "federal") to be gathered just outside Paris. The King refused to sanction this, and when Roland urged him to prove his patriotism by accepting the decrees penalizing priests and establishing the federal force, Louis XVI dismissed both Roland and Clavière. Widening controversy over the decree calling for federal troops led to the demonstration of June 20, 1792, on the third anniversary of the Tennis Court Oath (and the first anniversary of the King's flight). An immense crowd, including armed National Guard battalions, filed peacefully but noisily through the Tuileries palace past Louis XVI, who was wearing a tricolor cockade. The politics of the summer of 1792 grew increasingly heated over the issues raised in June.

The Paris Sections' Petition
for Dethronement of Louis XVI

There was a regular and lawful procedure for obtaining the views of the sections of Paris under the constitutional monarchy, and this procedure was invoked by the Fontaine-de-Grenelle section on July 19, 1792. It proposed to the other forty-seven sections of Paris the preparation of a joint address to the departmental administrations throughout the country and also an address to the National Legislative Assembly asking that, in taking measures to meet the national emergency, the Assembly consider only "the supreme law of the People's Salvation." As the Fontaine-de-Grenelle section requested, the municipal administrators of Paris thereupon convoked representatives of all the sections, who met during the last week of July and the first three days of August, with Collot d'Herbois presiding and Audouin as one of the secretaries. An address to the National Legislative Assembly was prepared, read to the Assembly on August 3 by the mayor, Pétion, and ordered to be printed, with the signatures of the representatives of forty sections. (Representatives of seven other sections signed it during the ensuing three days.)

The text was printed accurately in various pamphlets and the newspaper *Moniteur*; one of the pamphlets, *Les voeux du véritable souverain*, contains a footnote signed by Pétion, which is included here.

Legislators, when our country is in danger all her children ought to come together quickly in her defense; and never has so great a peril threatened our country. The commune of Paris sends us to you; we are coming to present in the laws' sanctuary the wishes of an immense city. Imbued with respect for the nation's representatives, full of confidence in their courageous patriotism, it has not despaired of the public salvation; but it believes that, to heal the ills of France, they must be attacked at the source and not a moment must be lost. With grief, it hereby denounces the chief of the executive power. . . .

We shall not retrace for you the entire conduct of Louis XVI since the first days of the revolution, his bloody projects against the city of Paris, his predilection for nobles and priests, the aversion he showed to the mass of the people, [nor] the National Constituent Assembly outraged by court valets, surrounded by armed men, wandering in the middle of a royal city, and finding asylum only in a tennis court. We shall not retrace for you oaths so many times violated, protestations ceaselessly renewed and ceaselessly belied by actions, until the moment when a perfidious flight opened the eyes even of the citizens who had been most blinded by the fanaticism of slavery. We shall leave aside all that is covered by the people's pardon; but to pardon is not to forget. Besides, it would be in vain to try to forget all these misdeeds; they will soil the pages of history, and posterity will remember them.

However, legislators, it is our duty to remind you briefly of the benefits that the nation has conferred on Louis XVI and the ingratitude of that prince. How many reasons there are to remove him from the throne at the moment when the people have reconquered sovereignty! The memory of an imperious and devouring dynasty, in which there were twenty tyrants as against one king, the hereditary despotism growing from reign to reign with the people's misery, the public finances entirely ruined by Louis XVI and his two predecessors, infamous treaties ruining the national honor, the eternal enemies of France becoming her allies and masters: those were the rights of Louis XVI to the constitutional scepter. The nation, faithful to its character, has chosen to be generous rather than prudent; the despot of a slave land has become the king of a free people; after having attempted to flee from France in order to reign over Coblenz, he has been placed on the throne again, perhaps against the wishes of the nation which should have been consulted. . . .

And all the benefits conferred by the nation were soon turned against it. The power delegated to Louis XVI to maintain liberty has been armed to overthrow it. Cast a glance upon the interior of the Empire. Perverse ministers are removed by the irresistible force of public scorn; they are the ones whom Louis XVI regrets. Their successors inform the nation and the king of the danger which surrounds our country; they are dismissed by Louis XVI for having shown themselves to be citizens. Royal inviolability and perpetual changes in the ministry let the agents of the executive power elude their responsibility. A conspiratorial guard is dissolved in appearance, but it still exists; it is still in the hire of Louis XVI; it sows trouble and will harvest civil war. Priests, as agitators, abusing their power over timid consciences, arm sons against fathers and, from the sacred land of liberty, send new soldiers to march under the banners of servitude. These enemies *of the people* are protected by the appeal *to the people,* and Louis XVI maintains their right to conspire. . . .

From without, enemy armies threaten our territory. Two despots publish against the French nation a manifesto as insolent as it is absurd. Treasonous Frenchmen, led by the King's brothers, relatives, allies, are preparing to tear the country bodily apart. Already the enemy, on our frontiers, sends executioners against our warriors. . . .

A minister's exaggerated promises have caused war to be declared, and we have begun it with our armies incomplete and bare of all they need. In vain Belgium appeals to us; perverse orders have shackled the ardor of our soldiers; our first steps in those fair lands have been marked by the fire of domestic strife, and the arsonist is still in the camp of the French. All the decrees that the National Assembly has enacted to reinforce our troops are annulled by the refusal of sanction or by perfidious delays. And the enemy is advancing with great strides while patricians are commanding the armies of equality; while our generals are leaving their post in the face of the enemy and letting the armed force adopt and come to present to the legislators its wishes, which it cannot legally express, and slander a free people, which it is in duty bound to defend.

The chief of the executive power is the main link in the counter-revolutionary chain. He seems to participate in the plots of Pillnitz, which he has so tardily made known. His name struggles against that of the nation; his name is a signal for discord between the people and its magistrates, between the soldiers and the generals. He has separated his interests from those of the nation. We, too, separate them. Far from having opposed by any formal act the enemies without and within, his conduct is a perpetual and formal act of disobedience to the constitution. As long as we have such a king, freedom cannot grow strong; and we want to remain free. Out of a remnant of indulgence, we would have desired to be able to ask you to suspend Louis XVI for as long as the danger to our country exists; but that would be unconstitutional. Louis XVI ceaselessly invokes the constitution; we invoke it in our turn, and we ask you to depose him.

This great measure once carried, as it is very doubtful that the nation can have confidence in the present dynasty, we ask that ministers, responsible as a group, named by the National Assembly but outside its membership, in accordance with constitutional law, named by free men, by voice vote, wield executive power provisionally while waiting for the will of the people, our sovereign and yours, to be legally pronounced in a national convention as soon as the security of the State permits. Meanwhile, let all our enemies, whoever they may be, form ranks beyond our frontiers; let the weak and the forsworn abandon freedom's soil; let three hundred thousand slaves come forward; they will find before them ten million free men,[1] as ready for death as for victory, fighting for

[1] The latest counts and calculations of the population of France put the number of inhabitants at 27 million, among whom there are 10 million males between 16 and 90 years of age . . . , of whom 6,700,000 are capable of bearing arms, viz.: 2,880,000 active citizens [each paying a tax of at least 1½ *livres* a year and thus having the right to vote] and 3,820,000 passive citizens [non-voters].

France is internally divided into two quite distinct parties, one commonly referred to as the *honnêtes gens* [decent, respectable people] and the other as the *sans-culottes* [no breeches; hence, wearing the long trousers of the working-man]. These parties are stirring up the kingdom and are ready to turn France over to the horrors of a civil war. As combat between the two parties can

equality, for their homes, their wives, their children, and their old people. Let each of us be a soldier in turn; and if we are to have the honor of dying for our country, let each of us, before breathing his last, make his memory illustrious for the death of a tyrant or a slave.

Proceedings of the Quinze-Vingts Section

Most of the direct evidence concerning political opinion in the various sections of Paris in 1792 was destroyed by fire in 1871. It is still demonstrable that they were not unanimous. The Mauconseil section, having considered in its assembly of July 31 that in providing for the monarchy of Louis XVI the Constitution "cannot be recognized as the expression of the general will . . . that Louis XVI has lost the nation's confidence," solemnly declared that it no longer recognized him as king and retracted its oath of loyalty to him; it proposed to march to the National Assembly on August 5 to announce this. The historian Braesch showed that during the next four days, the Arsenal, Henri IV, Temple, and Jardin-des-Plantes sections reacted with disapproval; the historian Mortimer-Ternaux, who saw documents later destroyed, had asserted that twelve other sections also rejected the Mauconseil decision while fourteen accepted it.

The atmosphere of one Paris section can to some extent be re-

take place only if they are of equal strength, it is necessary to acquaint them with the disproportion that exists.

All the passive citizens are in the *sans-culottes'* party, thus 3,820,000 men.

Among the active citizens there are 1,680,000 citizens with little property, thus 1,680,000 of the *sans-culottes'* party.

The 1,200,000 active citizens with more property include 30,000 men of great wealth and 70,000 of moderate wealth. The 1,100,000 remaining are divided into three classes, viz.: 300,000 of the *honnêtes gens'* party, 400,000 uncertain, and 400,000 of the *sans-culottes'* party.

In summary, the proportion of the *sans-culottes* to the *honnêtes gens* is about fifteen to one. It follows that it is wholly impossible for civil war to break out or for one party to attack the other; the disproportion is too great, and it is extremely probable that the weak party will join the other against the common enemy, either external or internal.

Calculations from much more accurate data, based on many considerations, prove that among the 180,000 [potential] combatants in Paris there are 20,000 for the party referred to as the *honnêtes gens* and 160,000 for the other; it is therefore impossible that there could be civil war in Paris, as the common enemy desires.

Pétion, mayor.

captured in the excerpts that follow, from the minutes of proceedings of the Quinze-Vingts section, published by Buchez and Roux, *Histoire parlementaire de la Révolution française* (Paris, 1834-1838), XVI, 403-408, as corrected by Mortimer-Ternaux, *Histoire de la Terreur* (Paris, 1862-1869), II, 236.

August 3, 1792

A deputation from Saint-Marcel came to ask their brothers of the faubourg Saint-Antoine to march with them, armed, next Sunday, the 5th of this month, to the National Assembly. By unanimous agreement of all the citizens composing the sectional assembly, it was decided:

1. That they would assemble promptly at nine o'clock in the morning on the Place de la Bastille, with the citizens of the faubourg Saint-Marcel;

2. That the drums would beat general quarters in the morning;

3. That the commissioners named by it will inform the forty-seven other sections, which will be asked to send notice of their wishes to the assembly tomorrow evening, inviting them to join, with arms, and march together; and it has named, for this purpose, citizens Desesquelle and Huguenin.

4. It has appointed citizens Duclos, Carré, Menant, and Leduc to inform its brothers the Marseillais of this and invite them to join, with arms.

The section then passed on to other subjects . . . it decided that any man nominated by the active citizens residing for one year in the territory of the section would be admitted into its battalion. [signed] Huguenin, president; Desesquelle, secretary.

August 4, 1792

Adoption of the minutes of the evening before.

Immediately there appeared Osselin, municipal officer, accompanied by four commissioners appointed by the commune, who brought a letter from the mayor, in which they joined, to engage the citizens not to take an unconsidered step tomorrow but to await the National Assembly's action on the petition from the commune of Paris in its forty-eight sections.

The assembly, feeling the justice of the views presented by the mayor and the officers sent by him to the assembly, decided that it would retract its decision of yesterday, as applied to tomorrow, that it would wait patiently, peaceably, and watchfully, until next Thursday at eleven o'clock in the evening, for the action of the National Assembly; but that if justice and right are not done to the people by the legislative body before Thursday at eleven o'clock in the evening, then at midnight the tocsin will ring and the drums will sound general quarters and everyone will rise up at the same time.

Immediately Carré, Rossignol, Doinet, and Balin were named commissioners for the purpose of taking the foregoing resolutions to our brothers of the faubourg Saint-Marcel, and Fournereau was named commissioner for the purpose of taking the same resolution to our brothers the Marseillais right away.

At this instant Huguenin, president, and Desesquelle, secretary, being tired, left the session and were replaced at once, by acclamation, by Lebon as president and Renet as secretary. . . . [signed] Desesquelle; Huguenin.

August 9, 1792

Commissioners arrived from the sections Poissonnière, Bonne-Nouvelle, Gobelins, Montreuil, Gravilliers, Beaubourg, Ponceau, Croix-Rouge, Lombards, Mauconseil, Popincourt, Arsenal, and Tuileries, which all agree with the decisions of the Quinze-Vingts section, recognizing that they are calculated to save and ensure the public weal.

A federal, speaking in behalf of his brothers, requested the assembly to maintain its decision of the 4th.

A letter was read from the federals of the eighty-two departments, asking to be allowed to join the inhabitants of the Quinze-Vingts section, under the same flags, to defend and save our country. A member's proposal, to deliver to the citizens of the section twenty-four muskets, was enthusiastically accepted.

It was decided, in order to save our country, and as proposed by a member of a section of Paris, that three commissioners would be named by each section, to join the commune and advise on prompt means to save the public weal, and for this purpose it was decided that orders would be taken only from the assembled commissioners of the majority of sections. To represent the Quinze-Vingts section, Rossignol, Huguenin, and Balin were named.

Then the tocsin was heard to ring. The assembly, having received no order with reference to this from the commissioners sent to join the commune, charged Bouthidon and Carré to stop this awful signal, which was done for some time. But having heard the drums beat general quarters and the tocsin ring in the city, the assembly was not able to prevent it from being rung an hour later. At this moment the assembly declared itself to be in continuous session.

After the session was declared continuous, a letter arrived from Rossignol, one of the commissioners in the city hall, requesting that the tocsin be delayed until the commissioners who have come together from the sections have taken the steps necessary in the circumstances. A member proposed having the battalion assemble under arms, and the assembly, in the person of its president, ordered the second-in-command of the said battalion to have it march to the place where our country's danger calls its defenders. Done [signed] Miette, secretary.

A Letter from a Federal Volunteer

Obeying a decree adopted by the National Assembly in May, despite the royal veto applied to it, the administrative authorities of the district and municipality of Brest, like those in a number of other localities, assembled at the end of June to organize the raising of a company of volunteers. The battalion of federal troops from the Finistère department, numbering somewhat more than 100 men, arrived in Paris on July 24. They were under the command of Pierre-François Desbouillons, a 27-year-old former clerk in the port of Brest, who quickly came to the conclusion that the King had to be deposed, as he wrote two days later in a report to the

100   THE CAPTURE OF THE TUILERIES PALACE, 1792

authorities in Brest; on the other hand, observation of the National Assembly led him to regret the confusion of its debates, the
inattention of the legislators, and their tendency to exchange
personal insults. On August 10, in the afternoon or evening,
Desbouillons wrote the following report to Brest on the events of
that day.

His letter was edited by Max-Hervé Thomas in *Information
Historique*, XXI (1959), 182-183.

Administrators,

I shall not undertake to answer today the letter you wrote on the
3rd to the division I command, because what has happened here
since the last mail will sufficiently prove to you that, if my comrade
and I did not take the oath which you, and we, disapprove, we
nonetheless thought, rightly, that the real danger was in Paris and
that our presence here was necessary.

Feeling was running so high in the capital that every day some
violent crisis was expected. As you know, the plot to assassinate the
mayor had been discovered, and since then every day we provided
him with a more or less heavy guard. The detachment that reported
to him day before yesterday has not yet been relieved as of the
time I am writing to you and consequently was not able to take
part in the business of which I am going to give you the details.

The people, tired of the Assembly's feebleness and convinced by
what its most distinguished members said that only the people
could save our country, had decided, in certain sections of the
faubourgs, on a new insurrection Thursday evening at midnight,
in case at that hour the Assembly had still not voted to depose the
King. No argument was capable of diverting them from this plan.
Yesterday, then, at the stroke of midnight, general quarters was
being drummed and the tocsin was ringing in almost all parts of
the city.

We at once took up arms and, in accordance with the written
order from the Gobelins section, we went to join the Saint-Marceau
battalion. Its commander sent to the different parts of the city to
find out what was happening in them. We found out that all the
battalions, under arms, were remaining in their respective headquarters. It was agreed that we would join with the Cordeliers'
battalion, and at dawn we started off. We took with us that battalion, joined by the intrepid Marseillais, and we made our way to

the Tuileries, where we found a few battalions. We lined up in battle formation on the Place du Carrousel. We remained there a long time without knowing what to do.

There was no definite plan, no recognized chief. With several of my comrades, I did everything I could to bring about a meeting of the chiefs of the various battalions so that they would give someone the general command. The chiefs met, but our efforts were in vain, for almost at once they dispersed without having a definite plan; we all knew it was necessary to attack the Tuileries palace, which was filled with armed men and had all its gates closed. The rumor spread that twenty-two armed royalists had just been arrested, and soon afterward the head of one of them was to be seen in our midst. Yet we remained in a state of inaction. We were few in number on the Place du Carrousel, and we did not know whether on the other sides [of the palace] they were in greater strength.

The palace court was filled with cannon and cannoneers of the national guard. We had opportunities to notice this because several times the gate had been opened to let a few persons in or out. As for us, soldier citizens, we had steadfastly been refused entry. A few hotheads decided to force the gate. Axes were raised, broke it, and at once knocked it down. A few persons ventured into the court. Guardsmen came towards them, raising their hats. They embraced, and the guardsmen came over. Several times the national guard which was guarding the palace was urged to imitate them. Part of it yielded and joined us in taking away the cannon that were in the court. I forgot to mention that as soon as the gate to the court was knocked down, cannoneers were so intrepid as to go in with one of their pieces, which they dragged to the middle of the court and aimed at the palace door. There still remained a few artillery pieces in the entrance hall, but there was no attempt to remove them.

But immediately men went in and part way up the steps on which the Swiss had barricaded themselves. Every effort was made to get them to leave that position and join us. No one had any intention other than to disarm them. They steadfastly refused to give in to our urgent attempts at persuasion. One of them decided to come alone to speak to the national guard and was descending the steps when men doubtless assigned and paid to start the conflict tried to stab him. At once he rejoined his comrades. Everyone was still conferring. A musket shot had been fired without starting the fighting. The commanders of the Swiss and other generals persisted in saying that without an order from the King they would not leave their posts. "Then you all want to die," someone said to them. "Yes," they replied, "we shall all die rather than abandon our posts without an order from the King."

The area around the bottom of the staircase was filled with citizens, most of whom had only sabers. In the moving about, one of the Swiss leaders was slightly cut, and at once these citizens were generally and overwhelmingly fired on. Battle was joined everywhere, and scenes of horror multiplied on every hand. Unfortunately not all the battalions of the national guard were on our side: several remained inactive at the beginning of the affair, and I have even been assured that some fired on their fellow citizens.

The Swiss made a sortie which at first carried all before it, but instantly they were counter-charged and everywhere forced back [into the court]. Some laid down their arms; others fled and closed themselves up in the palace, from which they continued to fire. Then the artillery was brought into the court and cannon were discharged everywhere; the palace was entered and those who were defending themselves in it were exterminated. Those who had fled toward the Champs-Élysées, who included the leaders, encountered a battalion of citizens who stopped them. They formed a battle square and delivered terrific fire from that position. At once the cannon was brought up, and they were overwhelmed. Few escaped, and we had a complete victory, but it was deadly for us.

Mingle your tears with ours; they are still flowing at this moment. Our brothers Benthomme and Kéréon are dead, and up to now we know of two wounded. . . . Neither is dangerously wounded. . . . We withdrew about one o'clock in the afternoon; battalions of the national guard were then arriving; we were exhausted, many of us, myself included, not having slept at all for three days. We had something to eat and drink and went straight to bed, from which we are now getting up. When we left the Place du Carrousel, the buildings which separate it from the palace court were on fire. We left to those who came after us the task of putting it out. We did not then know of the march of the Swiss from Courbevoie, or we would have forgotten our fatigue and run to meet them. Many traitors have been found in the ranks; justice has quickly been done to those who were recognized; several persons have been hanged or beheaded for taking things from the palace.

The mail is about to leave; I cannot write you at greater length.

At this moment, I have learned that a certain Maisonneuve was shot in the shoulder, but there is no fear for his life.

A Letter from a Legislator

> The writer of the following letter, Michel Azéma, was a land-owner, 40 years old, from a village near Narbonne. Before the Revolution, he had been admitted to law practice. He was elected to the administrative directory of the Aude department in 1790 and to the National Legislative Assembly in 1791. In this letter, completed in the early hours of August 11, 1792, he reported to his former colleagues in Carcassonne on the events he had just witnessed.
>
> The letter was edited by Camille Bloch in *Révolution Française,* XXVII (1894), 177-182.

Paris
August 10, midnight, in session
the 4th year of liberty, 1792

My prophecies are proving only too true; abuses can't last . . . The people are the same today as on July 14, 1789; the second Bastille, the Tuileries palace, was forced open and taken as promptly as the famous Bastille at Saint-Antoine. The Revolution's worst enemy . . . —the veto, using the Constitution as a pretext to destroy the Constitution—had long been a grievance; the evil was tolerated patiently as long as the majority of the National Assembly showed itself; but it was intolerable as soon as, in the La Fayette business, fear, etc., gave the black or vetoizing side a majority, 406 votes to 224. Despair led to rough treatment of several deputies leaving that disastrous session.

The indignation was so general that it was breaking out with no fear or restraint; everyone was expecting a terrible explosion; day and night, the palace was filled with brave and valorous knights,

was bristling with bayonets, cannon, etc. Yesterday the fears inten-
sified; still, no reason for it appeared in actuality, so just after midnight we went to bed.

About two hours later they came to call me, as well as the other
deputies nearest the Assembly hall; the tocsin was ringing on all
sides, the drums were beating the general alarm everywhere, but no
assemblage appeared anywhere. Order reigned everywhere; there
was complete tranquillity all over Paris, so that, about six o'clock in
the morning, the session was recessed, though it did not disperse.

I took advantage of this moment to check up for myself on the
state of the capital; I saw the Place Vendôme, which faces our so-
called Feuillants' door, covered with National Guardsmen, cannon,
etc.; all around the palace there were equally many defenders,
cannon muzzles, etc. I pushed on with my inspection, in the cool
of early morning, along the quais to the Pont-Neuf and the Place
de Grève; I inspected the city hall, the great Market, and came
home by way of the Place des Victoires, the Rue Neuve des Petits
Champs [subsequently renamed Rue des Petits Champs and, at the
western end, Rue Danielle Casanova] and the boulevard [de la
Madeleine]. Everywhere I was satisfied to see complete calm, so
much so that I was angry with those who had called out the deputies
and with the ringers of tocsins and the drummers of general
quarters. But this apparent calm was the one that comes before
the most furious tempests.

I dressed up and had a big breakfast, fortunately; in that time I
saw, on the boulevard under my windows, a small collection of
men armed with pikes, muskets, and sabers, with women mingled
among them but with two cannon in front, all coming from the
faubourg Saint-Antoine and going towards the National Assembly.
Knowing the security measures taken everywhere wholly reassured
me.

Shortly afterward, my appetite disappeared at the passage of a
second troop similar to the first one; finally, the men from Marseilles and other federals went by, and I hurried to my post, about
seven o'clock in the morning. On the way, I saw the stations all
garrisoned and the National Guard quiet; but having arrived at
our Feuillants' door, I found it impossible to get through the
crowd of wild men who were tearing seventeen former King's
Guards, arrested during the night by the patrols around the

Tuileries, away from the guards on duty and briskly dispatching them to their glory.

Having entered the Assembly by the so-called Capucins' door, I was greatly surprised to find the King, the Queen, the Prince, the King's oldest sister, and Madame Elisabeth, etc., etc., all very carelessly dressed, with heads lowered like whipped dogs; they had all taken refuge in the midst of the National Assembly to seek there the salvation no longer to be found in their palace, despite all the Don Quixotes in it armed with everything but courage. The cannoneers, on being urged to really do their duty against the people if they should force a way into the palace, had simply unloaded their cannon, so that the gentlemen of the Department, and Pétion, etc., who were among the first to run to the King, had advised him to come amongst the nation's representatives.

The National Assembly was not deliberating; it could not in the King's presence, but it urgently needed to do so. The King and the royal family could not be sent out, because they were done for if they left their asylum. After great and tumultuous debate, the King moved from the President's left and his family moved from inside the rail, to be placed in the little box used by journalists taking notes on debates behind the President and to his right.

Someone came to announce to us that the cannon filling the Place du Carrousel were aimed against the Tuileries palace, which the people wanted to break down like the Bastille. After a short discussion, because time was pressing, it was decreed to send a deputation of twenty members of the Assembly to the people, to speak to them in the name of the law and to appease them by persuasion. To hasten the choice, the president was authorized to make it. At once, the deputation left, in double file, preceded by an usher and surrounded by a guard. I had the honor, which was at the same time almost a misfortune, to be in it; we had barely arrived at the door of the palace towards the Tuileries [gardens] when our eyes were dazzled by furious musket fire at the bottom of the stairway; at once, a second round; then a cannonade knocked down part of the façade. My word! Death was right before us; but, as it was unworthy to put it behind us, we contented ourselves with stopping; we moved the previous question, but a majority of well-aimed cannon rejected it. We thought we had a safe alternative in going to the other side of the Carrousel, preferring the cannon tails to the mouths; but scarcely had we emerged from the riding-school [in which the Assembly met] when a mass of sabers, pikes, and bayonets rushed from all sides, with indescribable rage, on our brave guards, who, finally provoked by our obstinacy in going forward instead of back, grabbed us and swooped back with us into the National Assembly.

We were reporting on our fine exploits, our fortunate success, when the artillery thundered outside the Assembly; at this critical moment, whatever else may be said about it, we all sprang up, raised our arms and hats in the air, and made the hall echo with our shout, "Vive la nation!" We then stood still, our bodies, not our hearts, for to judge by mine they were palpitating in all the members present (there were at least 200 absent). Above all, we were listening intently, awaiting the reality of the thundering noise and even more of the hail.

Brave *sans-culottes* fortunately appeared at the rail; they got a very prompt hearing. They notified us that the sovereign people was using its sovereignty and had charged them to assure us of its respect, to affirm obedience to our decrees, which it was sanctioning despite the traitorous veto, and that we were the only constituted authority and there was no other in existence. They concluded, "Swear in the Nation's name to maintain liberty and equality with all your power or to die at your post."

No one answered, because that was the price and the only means of our salvation; all the deputies, *una voce dicentes,* shouted, with eagerness, by acclamation, with joy, unanimously and simultaneously; "I so swear!" We rapidly adopted the form of words, the roll was called at once, and on the rostrum each in turn pronounced the words indicated by the *sans-culottes* and adopted. Our co-deputies, absent and scared to death, reassured by a declaration so easy to pronounce, without troubling over the difficulty and even, for most of them, the impossibility of carrying it out, came back, fresh and alert, to join us in session and to show the utmost courage in taking this charming oath, which they uttered with the greatest firmness.

Meanwhile, a great brawl was going on in the palace, in the Tuileries [gardens], on the Champs Élysées; and the Swiss who had been deceived by the aristocratic instigators in the palace and had fired first on the people, especially on the brave Marseillais running

to embrace them after false assurances of friendship and brotherhood, were being hotly pursued and were defending themselves
in the same way, everywhere in the Tuileries gardens, in the palace,
and around it; the ground is still to be seen covered with corpses.

It is impossible to calculate the number of dead and wounded.
. . . As for me, having been everywhere this evening, seen everything and heard everything myself, and compared and evaluated
everything, I place the number of dead at about seven to eight
hundred on each side, and as many wounded, and do not think I
am wrong by much. All the buildings connected to the palace were
set on fire; but the people, reversing their course, asked the firemen
to put out the fire and prevent it from spreading into the palace
and offered to help the firemen; which is now being done zealously.
The palace was pillaged, devastated, but everything of value was
carried scrupulously to the Assembly, which has sent it to the
Commune [i.e., city-hall]; the people themselves did justice to
those who concealed or stole the smallest thing from the odious
Veto; all the jewels, money, etc., found on the Swiss who were
killed have been carefully gathered up; a true sans-culotte has faith-
fully deposited 173 gold louis [equivalent to 3,460 livres] found on
a fanatical abbot of the palace, who was discovered in a basement.
Our sovereigns, truly French, have respected the ladies of honor,
or non-honor, of the court; they have not inflicted the least scratch
on them, ugly as certain of them may be; but no mercy has been
shown the knights obsequious to the court who were poisoning and
infesting it.

The King has been suspended from all his functions and powers;
we have driven out his counterrevolutionary ministers and have
named others, worthy of public confidence, etc. You will see all
the decrees we adopted today, so I'll not discuss their provisions
at length; we have taken almost the same measures as our Con-
stituents at the time of the King's escape, except for the National
Convention that we are asking the French people to form. Louis,
Antoinette, their children and hangers-on are still in their cell,
the stenographer's box, from which they have not budged, in
which close by one another, they have done all their unloading,
which cannot have been increased by their fare as this has consisted, deliberately, of scarcely more than bread, wine, and water.
Good God, what a sight! It is really true that opinion is often all-

important and that without opinion on their side the great, however great they may be, are nothing; these gods on earth, stripped and deprived of their masks, above all of the blind and stupid credulity of others, are not even men, and in the end they have the same fate that false divinities have always had when the blindfolds of error fall away. Our assembly-hall commissioners are taking steps to prepare apartments for them in the former Capucins' convent [next to the assembly-hall on the west]; for their majesties would run the risk of not being respected as they deserve if they were to go and stay in the Luxembourg palace, which one of our decrees assigned to them today instead of the Tuileries palace.

We're in continuous session; but two sleepless nights are making my eyelids droop and forcing me into a deep sleep, which I am going to try to find on a bench, two o'clock in the morning.

The Narrative by the Minister of Justice

One of the six ministers under the constitutional monarchy was the keeper of the seals, or minister of justice. In July and early August, this position was occupied by Étienne-Louis-Hector Dejoly. After August 10, in prison, he wrote two memoranda: first, on August 14, a circumstantial account of events on the night of August 9-10; then, later in August, a defense of his political conduct, which is long and repetitious but contains details important as background for his narrative.

This second memorandum mentions that Dejoly was 37 years old, a native of Montpellier, a lawyer in Paris from 1780 onward, having purchased in 1786, for 50,000 *livres,* the right to practice before the royal privy council. It recalls the political events of 1787 and 1788, the election of Dejoly to the provisional municipality of Paris on July 13, 1789, his subsequent service as one of its secretaries, his appointment as clerk of the constitutional municipality, where he was still serving in June, 1792. After the disorders of June 20, the National Legislative Assembly created the position of secretary of the council of royal ministers, and one of the ministers recommended him for the post because he was experienced, was not given to "excesses," and was not a member of a political club. Dejoly's memorandum says he later learned "that in appointing me to that position, the King intended to choose a man who might be acceptable" to the Assembly. Then, upon the resignation of the minister of justice, early in July, Dejoly was appointed to that position. He tried to get the council of ministers to restore Pétion as mayor and Manuel as executive officer of the Paris municipality (both had been suspended by the departmental administration for alleged complicity in the disorders of June 20; both were restored to office, but by action of the Assembly, not the council of ministers). Dejoly urged the King to appear before the National Assembly: "I wanted him to act as a prudent and constitutional king," he recalled. He advised the King to call in the mayor of Paris and the executive officer of the departmental administration, Roederer, to sit in the council of ministers.

Dejoly's memorandum says that he was cooperating with Roederer, who was friendly with influential members of the Assembly and was closely linked with Pétion. Together, Dejoly and Roederer suggested appointing to the council of ministers Camus, Tronchet, Fréteau, and Rabaut de Saint-Étienne, who had been notable members of the first (National Constituent) Assembly in 1789-1791. Dejoly's suggestions for winning the confidence of the current Assembly were opposed by the minister of naval and maritime affairs, Dubouchage, and in the end were rejected by the King. Discouraged by this and pessimistic over the political situation, Dejoly submitted his resignation on August 3. It was not acted on. Anxiety in the palace on August 4 led the ministers to agree to spend the ensuing night there, during which alarming reports came in. The King ordered Dejoly to notify the mayor, but ultimately it became clear that the troop movements were simply a transfer of the Marseilles battalion to another part of the city. On August 5, Dejoly's second memorandum says, it was too late for him to insist on giving effect to his resignation: "the peril was imminent, and it would have been weak and cowardly to abandon the post; so I stayed."

Dejoly's "Récit historique des faits qui se sont passés aux Tuileries dans la nuit du 9 au 10 août et dans la matinée du 10," written on August 14, 1792, was printed by Montjoie, in his *Histoire de Marie-Antoinette* (1797), pp. 367-396, and in a scholarly edition by Jacques Godechot in *Annales Historiques de la Révolution Française*, XVIII (1946), 362-382; it is translated here with omissions.

I was in the palace, and this is what I saw. The King had been informed several days before of the means that were being employed to stir up the people. . . .

The movement had been delayed. The postponement of the question concerning General La Fayette, the delay in the debate on the question of deposing the King, and the decree which quashed the vote by the Mauconseil section retracting its oath of fidelity to the King appear to have been the causes.

. . . Various orders were adopted in Wednesday's session. The mayor was called to the Department [of Paris]. He was awaited, futilely, until midnight.

The next day, Thursday, new anxieties assailed the departmental administrators. It had constantly been said that the people's calm depended on the judgment of the question whether the King was to be deposed; the report on this was to be made on Thursday: it was ceaselessly repeated that if this question was not decided that day before midnight, the people would rise up in their entirety. The report was awaited. It was made by Condorcet; but the debate was postponed.

At first it was thought that this postponement would put off the execution of the projects which were supposed to be carried out on that day. Still, new precautions were taken: the mayor was called to the Department. On the day when the decree of indictment against La Fayette had been rejected, Pétion had written that he would use every means but that he could no longer answer for anything. It was desired to hear him on this important point. He came. Osselin, a municipal officer and administrator of the royal domain, was with him; two ministers attended that conference: I was one of them. Each reported what he knew, and the conclusion was that the evil was extreme, urgent, while the means to forestall or remedy it were almost nil.

The National Assembly had been affected by the rumors which concerned the Department and the ministers. The excesses to which various persons had gone the day before against several of its members, after the session in which the proposed indictment against La Fayette had been rejected, had drawn the attention of the legislative body. It had summoned the executive officer of the Department to report on the state of the capital as well as on the measures taken to ensure tranquillity. Roederer obeyed the decree. He concealed nothing. The National Assembly was informed.

Upon his return to the Department, Roederer found the mayor still there. The conference was resumed and continued heatedly; above all, it sought the means of restoring order, of calming emotions, of preventing all excesses. Persuasion was proposed by the mayor. The Department applauded this, and everyone promised to die at his post. But it was not sufficient to die. It was necessary to save the government.

It was then five o'clock. The ministers were receiving, hourly, new details on the plan and the time of its execution. These details appeared so terrifying, and their opinions so urgent, that three ministers went to the palace to communicate them to the King. . . .

Having informed the King, the Queen, and their family, the ministers withdrew to return an hour later. It was then nine o'clock in the evening. Each in his own department took the measures that prudence could suggest to him. Soon they came back to the palace. At ten o'clock they were all gathered there.

Before returning to the palace, I had gone to the Department. I had seen the executive officer. The Department was to remain assembled all night. The executive officer had offered to come and spend the night in the palace if the King thought it necessary. The King expressed the desire for it. I informed Roederer of this immediately, and that magistrate went to the King's presence. It was then nearly midnight.

It was the hour at which the assemblage was to form and the tocsin was to ring in several places. Faithful emissaries had been sent into several parts of the capital; and all who came in brought the most alarming news.

The assemblage was forming. Armed men had been running for two hours through the streets of the faubourg Saint-Antoine; others were waiting peaceably in their houses for the hour for assembly to come. Finally, the tocsin rang, and from everywhere they ran to the ground where the Bastille [demolished in 1789] had stood.

The square in front of the city hall was soon covered with a great number of persons. The general council of the Commune was assembled and, like the Department, it was arranging to spend the night.

Events had not yet gone so far, the tocsin had not rung, when the mayor and several municipal officers, among them Boucher, Borie, Therrein, Leroux, Vignier, left the city hall to go to the palace.

They were at once introduced into the King's presence. The mayor told him "that in the moment of crisis, the danger of which he was obliged not to conceal, he had hastened to come in person to see to the security of the King and the preservation of his family."

The King thanked Pétion in the most affectionate manner. The conversation lasted for a few minutes, and Pétion broke it off first, to go inspect the guards' posts.

He went down, in fact, into the court and the garden. He went to all the posts, spoke to the commanders, and came back on the terrace facing the palace, after having been to present himself at the rail of the National Assembly, where several deputies had gathered as soon as they had heard the drums beat, the tocsin ring and the alarm-cannon fire.

It was then one o'clock in the morning. The tocsin having begun to ring only after the mayor had left the King, the King charged me to inform Pétion of it and to express to him His Majesty's desire to have the gates closed to the Feuillants' terrace. . . .

Pétion received the King's observations, and he saw their soundness; before going to the National Assembly, he had the gate closed which leads to the court of the riding-school. The Swiss guard received the verbal order for it, in the presence of all the municipal officers and of various grenadiers who had accompanied the mayor.

I owe it to the truth to say that at this moment a grenadier let himself be carried away; his feelings prevailed over his obedience. "Monsieur mayor," he said, "we see with the keenest satisfaction, with a respectful gratitude, that your zeal still wins over the malevolence of your enemies, that you are everywhere where you can usefully serve our country. But that does not suffice. Why do you permit all these partial assemblages in Paris, which are leading to general ones? Why do you let yourself be dominated by factious men who will ruin us? Why, for example, is Santerre always with you, always out of reach of the law? Why, at this moment, is he at the city hall? Monsieur mayor, you are answerable for the public tranquillity, for the preservation of our properties, you. . . ." At these words, uttered with great excitement, which the mayor heard and to which he answered vaguely, "Sir, what is the meaning of this? You are forgetting respect, you are failing to observe propriety. Ah! let's see, let's be clear. . . ." At these words, I say, almost all the National Guardsmen pressed around the mayor, silenced the grenadier, forced him to withdraw, and the mayor went to the National Assembly; there he gave the clarifications that were asked of him, but he did not speak of the Feuillants' terrace.

The instant after, Pétion came back to the garden and returned on the terrace, and I saw him walk in the middle of the same group, accompanied by the same municipal officers and by a greater number of National Guardsmen. . . .

The King then had him requested to come up into the apartment. But the mayor thought that his presence was more necessary in the garden.

It was three-thirty. Messages were arriving one after another with the most alarming rapidity. Each one brought worse news than the last. Someone came to report to us that the city hall was filling with persons whose intentions appeared extremely hostile.

Soon after, they came to tell us that the municipality had been cancelled, dismissed; and its members, with the exception of Pétion and Manuel, replaced by citizens who said they had the general powers of the Commune; that, already, this provisional municipality had given orders and that it had just called Mandat, commander of the National Guard, who was being accused of having had Pétion detained on private business.

Mandat answered that his post was in the palace, that he was necessary, indispensable there; that he would, however, go to the city hall as soon as he could lay down the command.

A second order, which arrived at five o'clock in the morning, determined Mandat's departure. He left the palace, went to the city hall; there he was placed under arrest, and I have since found out that, the next day, about ten o'clock in the morning, while he was being taken to the Abbaye [prison], he became one of the victims of the people's fury and aberration.

The removal of Mandat left the command to La Chesnaye.

I then saw great activity in the palace.

The National Guardsmen, the Swiss guards were called to their posts. Each one reported there in the best order. The interior of the apartments, the stairways, the vestibules were staffed, the posts in the courts were divided up. The cannon were posted in different parts of the court; all these preparations heralded the most terrible intentions; they seemed to express the determination to set up a vigorous resistance. I turned my eyes away and moaned, first over the manner and then over the ineffectiveness of these preparations. Over the manner, since I was seeing prepared a scene of blood and murders without number; over the ineffectiveness, for despite this criminal, extravagant plan for an impossible resistance, I was convinced in advance that there would be no barrier powerful enough to stop the will of a people which was so determined to obtain what it had several times called for.

My opinion was strengthened when I saw the interior of the palace fill up with citizens armed and formed into troops whose spirit was evidently the same as that of the men who were regarded as the aggressors.

It was greatly strengthened when, at six o'clock in the morning, I saw a great number of armed citizens arrive in a body preceded by several cannon, line up in battle formation and in the best order on the Place du Carrousel, form ranks, place their cannon, halt, establish a command post, and stand at rest, which seemed destined to end only at the moment of attack.

I shall admit that until this last moment, I had retained some hope; I had thought that this day, which had been begun under such unfortunate auspices, would end in negotiations. But now I lost all hope.

I was of the opinion, since we could not have the municipality, to call the departmental council; I was thinking that it was appropriate to inform the National Assembly of what was happening, to ask it for help and protection; I proposed a letter to be written immediately by the King. But I still found opponents blocking me. The royal dignity would be impaired; the idea was unworthy of the Majesty of the throne. A letter from the minister of the Interior ought to suffice. Weak or perfidious councillors, it is thus that, for several days, you had been rendering futile all the efforts that might still have saved the State and your King.

In the end, this expedient was rejected. Two other plans were adopted.

The Department was called in, and it came at once to the palace. The minister of the Interior and I went to the National Assembly.

The minister of the Interior had written during the night to inform the legislative body of what was happening.

I obtained the floor and I reminded the National Assembly of this. Overwhelmed with grief, scarcely able to express myself, I announced that the worst was upon us, that the palace was surrounded, that it could be forced; that the least resistance could occasion the greatest misfortunes; that the ministers were no longer answerable for the preservation of the King's person; that they saw no means to save him except the sending of a deputation from the legislative body which would cover with its inviolability the

King and his family; that the King desired and was asking for this deputation, that he would never forget the fortunate effect that had been produced by a similar step on the day of June 20, and that he was sure that, in the present circumstances, the results would be as advantageous.

The National Assembly did not think that the circumstances were the same. On the one hand, the Assembly's attendance was not complete, and it could not deliberate. On the other hand, principles were invoked; they were regarded as controlling, and the deputation did not take place.

We withdrew at once; we encountered the Department [administrators, leaving the palace]; we informed them of our action; we got all its members to come to cover the King with the aegis of the law. The Department turned back [and] it arrived inside almost as quickly as we did. . . .

The King had been advised, and, while two of his ministers were at the National Assembly, two others had persuaded him to appear before the troops. He had gone down into the court; he had inspected all the guard-posts; he had seen all the battalions, inspected the Swiss guards, and had then gone back into the palace; he was proceeding through its interior. Everywhere, he said pleasant things, but I am assured that nowhere did he give orders.

The King had, then, witnessed the preparations that had been made. He saw the whole armed force ready for attack and defense, [and] he found almost two hundred persons attached to his service and to his court, whom an ill-advised zeal had brought to the palace, disposed to defend it. But he also saw that they were without arms. Scarcely were they armed with swords.

But they were lined up in rows three-deep, part in the reviewing hall, part in the gallery next to the billiard room. . . .

These preparations might have been good, the arrangements very sound. But their futility was demonstrated, as I had not ceased to say, and soon it was necessary to give them up.

Soon! At that very moment. The members of the Department and the two municipal officers who had remained in the palace, Borie and Leroux, had resolved to approach the people, to see them, to confer with them, to bring them, if possible, to a compromise. . . . [The effort to confer failed in the face of silence from the crowd. The members of the Department rejoined the royal ministers.]

With one accord, all urged the King to save himself and his family, to take refuge in the midst of the National Assembly. "It is only there, Sire," said Roederer, "amid the people's representatives, that Your Majesty, the Queen, the royal family can be secure. Come, let us fly: another quarter of an hour and the retreat will no longer be open to us." [Discussion.]

"Let us go," said the King, raising his right hand; "let us proceed, and since it is still necessary, let us give this last sign of devotion."

The Queen was brought along. . . .

"Monsieur Roederer, gentlemen," said the Queen, "you are answerable for the King's person; you are answerable for my son's."

"Madame," said Roederer, "we are answerable to the extent of dying at your side. That is all we can guarantee."

Military arrangements were made, at once, to protect the march from the palace to the National Assembly. The members of the Department formed a circle, in the middle of which the King, the Queen, the royal family, and Madame de Tourzel, governess of the royal children, took their places. . . .

In this order and with no further discussion, without having been able to take care of any needs, the procession passed through the rooms, went down the great stairway, and crossed the garden without encountering any obstacle.

At the other side of the terrace, by the Feuillants' café, we met a deputation of twelve members whom the National Assembly had sent to meet the King. The deputies mingled with the group that had formed inside the palace. They took the places of the members of the Department, who could not enter the assembly-hall. They protected the King's passage to the foot of the terrace.

The terrace was covered with people. Shouts of "Vive la Nation!" were mixed with "No veto!" The people appeared angry. Threatening expressions were addressed to the King and especially to the Queen: "No women," they were shouting from several parts of the terrace, "no women; we want only the King, the King alone!"

The executive officer of the Department was then authorized by the members of the deputation to have part of the King's Guards come up on the terrace. Once in command of this height, he

harangued the people; he told them that the National Assembly
had decided that it would receive the King and his family; he asked
for the carrying out of the decree. The people yielded to the law's
resolution. The King, the deputation, the royal family, went on
to the terrace and then into the Feuillants'. Entrance into the
assembly-hall was more difficult; it even became somewhat perilous.
The corridor was jammed. The National Guard could not get in;
it could not go back either. The march was interrupted. Shouts
were heard from all sides. However, the obstacles were removed.
The King was brought in, the Queen, the royal family, the ministers
followed him and the tumult ceased at the same time as the danger. . . .

The King spoke. He said: "Gentlemen, I come here to prevent a
great crime which might be committed; and I believe myself secure,
with my family and my children, when I am amidst the Nation's
representatives. I shall remain, with my ministers, until calm is
reestablished."

According to the Constitution, the King's presence paralyzed the
Assembly. It could no longer deliberate. But the circumstances were
urgent. It was impossible to place the King anywhere but in the
assembly-hall; it was still more impossible not to act at a moment
of extreme ferment. . . .

The Assembly soon decreed that the King and his family would
stay in the stenographer's box. They seated themselves there, in fact,
and from that moment the session resumed. It was then about nine-
thirty or ten o'clock in the morning.

I do not know what was happening outside. I could follow only
the movements inside. We had thought that after the King's with-
drawal, the people would be pacified; that if they took the palace,
they would have done so peaceably; that if they had demands, they
would address them to the National Assembly.

But oh, grief! At the moment when it was least expected, when
the members of the Department were presenting themselves at the
rail to report on the events of the night, several successive discharges of cannon and muskets were heard. Someone came to say
that the people, shot at by the Swiss, had assailed them in turn and
that they were wreaking dreadful carnage on them; that the people
had aimed their cannon at the palace, that they were intending to

knock it down, that they were firing indiscriminately on all whom they encountered in the apartments; that the palace, the garden, and the adjacent streets, as well as the square in front of the city hall, presented the horrible spectacle of a city taken by assault, whose inhabitants were being put to the sword.

Part Five
DEMOCRATIC GOVERNMENT AND REVOLUTIONARY WAR

The principal task of the National Convention, convoked in August and elected in September, 1792, was to draft a new constitution. It began united in the determination that France would be a republic. But thereafter it suffered from paralyzing clashes of personalities and factions which erupted over such issues as the fate of the deposed king, the relationship between the Convention and the city of Paris, and the nature of revolutionary legality. Meanwhile, there was a war to be fought and civil strife in a number of regions in France. These problems were met by waves of revolutionary legislation.

From late February to early April, 1793, the Convention instituted conscription for the army; established the special criminal court known as the "revolutionary tribunal" at Paris for trials of counter-revolutionaries, subversives, and conspirators; decreed the election of revolutionary surveillance committees in all the municipalities and every section of the large cities; regularized the assignment of three Convention members on mission with each of the armies; and created its own executive committee, the *Comité de salut public* (customarily referred to in English as the Committee of Public Safety, even though the word *salut* has the connotations of "salvation" and "welfare"). In connection with efforts to find accomplices of the traitorous General Dumouriez within the Convention, parliamentary immunity from arrest was abolished.

In the struggle between factions in the Convention, the municipality of Paris, the Jacobin club, and the majority of the sections in the city were by no means neutral. In mid-April, they called upon the Convention to eject 22 deputies, the most prominent of these being Brissot and Pétion. From May 19 onward, delegates from the sections met in the former episcopal palace hall (the Évêché) and formed a central revolutionary committee openly preparing for an insurrection in the capital. The Convention quickly elected a 12-member investigating commission, which ordered the arrest of a number of popular leaders. But on May 31, and again on June 2, the Convention was surrounded by armed men from the sections and the National Guard of Paris. They dispersed only after the Convention had voted for the arrest of 17 of the deputies named in April, ten members of the Commission of Twelve, and two other deputies, as well as the Minister of Finance and the Minister of Foreign Affairs.

The Convention rapidly submitted the democratic Constitution of 1793 to a referendum, and it was adopted in August. But it was not put into effect. The war and the threat of another insurrection in Paris led to another wave of revolutionary legislation, in which the principal measure was the law empowering local surveillance committees to order the arrest and detention of persons whose conduct, associations, writings, or conversations were suspect; the Convention's Committee on General Security was to review these orders.

The revolutionary government was given a kind of charter in the law of December 4, 1793 (14 frimaire, Year II, in the new non-Christian calendar). This was the work of the dominant faction known as the Mountaineers, who sat on the highest rows at the back of the hall and who prided themselves on the independence and equalitarianism of mountain men. This group itself was not united: in mid-January, 1794, one of its members, Dyzez, a former noble from the southwestern Landes department, wrote home, "I am constantly seeing the greatest ferment in the Mountain and also in the Jacobins' [club]. In both places there would long ago have been an explosion, without Robespierre."

The documents that follow include reports of two events which are in a formal way reminiscent of customary occurrences under the pre-revolutionary monarchy: the procession to celebrate a local festival and the edifying harangue by a leading member of a body exercising legislative and judicial powers. Other documents here provide typical examples of proceedings of the Convention and routine reports on public opinion in Paris; they all have to do with a single day, February 5, 1794 (17 pluviôse, Year II).

Inauguration of a Temple of Reason

In its incoming correspondence on February 5, 1794, the Convention received, from Pfliéger (a representative on mission with the Army of the Ardennes), a description of a civic festival held at Châlons-sur-Marne two weeks before. In the abbreviated version here, the speeches are omitted (for, as the president of the local *société populaire*, or Jacobin club, remarked, "Citizens, I am becoming wordy without noticing it. . . ."). This description has been published in the *Archives Parlementaires*, now edited by Reinhard and Bouloiseau (Paris, 1961-   ), LXXXIV, 298-302.

The festival was announced in the whole Commune the evening before; for this purpose, retreat was sounded by all the drummers and by the trumpeters of the troops in barracks at Châlons, in all parts of the town.

The next day at daybreak, it was again announced by general quarters, which was likewise sounded in all parts; the artillery did not fire, in order to save the powder to destroy the despots' henchmen.

The former church of Notre Dame was, for lack of time and means, cleaned and prepared only provisionally for its new use, and in its former sanctuary there was erected a pedestal supporting the symbolic statue of Reason. It is of simple and free design, decorated only by an inset bearing this inscription:

"Do unto others as you would have them do unto you."

It was flanked by two columns surmounted by two antique bronze perfume boxes, which emitted incense smoke during the whole ceremony: in front, at the foot of three steps, was placed an altar of antique form, on which were to be placed the emblems that the various groups composing the procession would put there; on the four pillars at the corners of the sanctuary were four projecting brackets to receive the busts of Brutus, the father of Republics and the model of Republicans; of Marat, the faithful friend of the people; of Le Peletier, who died for the Republic; and of the immortal Chalier.

At precisely nine o'clock in the morning, the general assemblage formed on the gravel promenade, otherwise called the promenade of Liberty; the military detachments and other groups destined to form the procession had their places indicated there; commissioners from the Society arranged them in order. . . .

Order of March

A detachment of cavalry, national constabulary, and hussars mingled together, to strengthen the bonds of fraternity, led the march, and on their pennant there were these words: "Reason guides us and enlightens us."

It was followed by the company of cannoneers of Châlons, preceded by a banner with this inscription: "Death to the Tyrants."

This company was followed by a cart loaded with broken chains, on which were six prisoners of war and a few wounded being cared for by a surgeon; this cart carried two banners, front and back, with these two inscriptions: "Humanity is a Republican virtue" [and] "They were very mistaken in fighting for tyrants."

This cart was accompanied by two detachments of national guardsmen and regular troops fully armed.

The drummers grouped together followed and in turn were followed by four *sans-culottes* carrying a superb fasces from which flew a tricolor banner on which were these words: "Let us be united like it, nothing can conquer us."

Forty women citizens dressed in white and decorated with tricolor ribbons surrounded the fasces, and each carried a large tricolor ribbon which was tied to her head.

A Liberty bonnet crowned this banner, and young national guardsmen accompanying the fasces carried various pennants on which were written different devices.

After them marched groups of national guardsmen and regular troops mingled together and fraternally and amicably united, arm in arm, singing hymns to Liberty and bearing with them two banners on which were written the following inscriptions: "Our Unity is our strength." "We will exterminate the last of the despots."

Then came the military band gathered from different barracks, playing alternately with the drummers who were in front during the procession. The band was followed by a chariot of antique type decorated with oak branches and bearing a sexagenerian couple, with a streamer on which were written these words: "Respect Old Age."

The Société Populaire marched next, preceded by its banner, on which was depicted a watchful eye, and underneath were these words: "We watch over the maintenance of Liberty and the public welfare."

In its train, groups of children of both sexes carried baskets of fruit and vases of flowers, accompanying a cart drawn by two white horses; in the cart was a young woman nursing an infant, beside her a group of children of different ages; it was preceded by a banner with this inscription: "They are the hope of the Patrie." From the cart flew a tricolor streamer with this inscription: "The virtuous mother will produce defenders for the Patrie."

Next marched a group of women citizens adorned with tricolor ribbons, bearing a standard with this inscription: "Austere Morals will strengthen the Republic." All who composed this group were dressed in white, as were the drivers of the cart, and all were bedecked with tricolor ribbons.

Then followed the surveillance committees of the sections of the Commune of Châlons, grouped together one after another; in front were four banners, each bearing the name of a section, and an emblem depicting a finger on the lips to indicate secrecy, and another banner with this inscription: "Our institution purges Society of a multitude of suspect people."

The Republic section went first; it accompanied a chariot pulled by two white horses and led by two men on foot dressed in Roman style; in it was a woman dressed in the same way, representing the Republic; on the front of this chariot appeared a tricolor ensign bearing these words: "Government of the Wise."

Next marched the Equality section, accompanying a plow pulled by two oxen and guided by a cultivator in work clothes; a couple seated on it carried a standard on which were written on one side,

"Honor the Plow," and on the other side, "Respect conjugal love."

The principal inspector and all the employees in the military storehouses formed a group which followed the plow: two standards were carried by this group; the first had the words, "Military supplies," and the second, "Our activity produces abundance in our armies."

The Liberty section followed, accompanied by groups of Citizens, artisans, and workmen of all kinds and types; each of them was carrying an instrument or a tool related to and representative of his art or occupation. This group was preceded by a tricolor standard, inscribed with a single word: "Sovereign."

Then marched the Fraternity section, consoling groups of convalescents, whose physicians were close by. In the middle of this section was an open cart from the Montagne hospital, containing men wounded in the defense of the Patrie, who appeared to have been cared for and bled by health officers who were binding their wounds. They were partly covered by their bloody bandages. The front of this cart carried a banner with this inscription: "Our blood will never cease to flow for the safety of the Patrie."

After the committees followed four women citizens dressed in white and adorned with tricolor belts decorated with the attributes of the four seasons they represented.

After the four seasons came the People's Representative in the midst of the constituted Authorities, civil and judicial, wearing their distinctive insignia. In their midst citizens carried litters draped in antique style and bearing the constitution and the busts of Brutus, Marat, Le Peletier, and Chalier. Each citizen held in his hand a wheat stalk, and on the banner which preceded the constituted Authorities was this inscription: "From the enforcement of the laws come prosperity and abundance."

The constituted Authorities were followed by various staff officers of the national guard of Châlons and by regular troops stationed in Châlons; they were preceded by a banner with this inscription: "Destroy the tyrants, or die."

Next, the natural children of the Patrie were led by a woman bearing a banner with this inscription: "The Patrie adopts us, we are eager to serve it."

Finally the old people, represented by veterans without weapons, formed a group preceded by two banners on which were these inscriptions: "The dawn of Reason and Liberty embellishes the end of our life" [and] "The French Republic honors loyalty, courage, old age, filial piety, misfortune; it places its constitution under the safekeeping of all the virtues."

After the group of veterans followed a cart drawn by four donkeys and containing remains of feudalism, such as armorial bearings, etc., as well as emblems of the superstition in which we were too long submerged. On the front was a man representing a pope adorned with tiara and pallium, having two cardinals for acolytes; on the front and rear of the cart were two billboards, the first of which bore the words "Prejudices pass away," and the second, "Reason is eternal."

The end of the procession was a detachment of cavalry, national guardsmen, and hussars mingled together, led by a trumpeter, and on their banner were these words: "The French government is revolutionary until the peace."

The whole being thus ordered, the procession left the promenade at exactly ten o'clock, crossed on the drawbridge, followed the avenue which is its continuation to reach the Rue de la Société Populaire, where there was a pause for the singing of . . . patriotic songs. . . . In the Place de la Liberté, there was another pause, for further singing. . . .

On the front steps of the city hall, there had been built and painted a mountain, at the top of which was placed a Hercules defending a fasces fourteen feet in height. A tricolor flag flew above it on which was written in large letters: "To the Mountain, the grateful French."

At the foot of the mountain, pure water flowed from a spring, falling by various cascades; twelve men dressed as mountaineers, armed with pikes and with civic crowns on their heads, were hidden in caverns in the mountain; as the procession arrived, singing the last couplet of the *Marseillaise,* the mountaineers quietly came out of their caverns without fully revealing themselves, and when "Aux armes, citoyens" was sung, they ran to get axes to defend their retreat, posted themselves on different sides of the mountain, but seeing the cart with feudalism and fanaticism drawn by asses with miters on their heads, they ran towards them, axe in hand, grabbed the miters, copes, and chasubles which adorned them as well as the pope and his acolytes, and chained them to the chariot of Liberty. During this, the band played a military charge; the carmagnole song was heard; but the mountaineers, seeing other carts arrive and feigning to believe that they were only the train following the one containing fanaticism, advanced in a column to meet the first one they saw, which was the chariot of Liberty; they lowered their axes as a sign of respect, and the band played a march; then a litter appeared, supporting a chair decorated with garlands; the Goddess descended from her cart, seated herself on the chair and was borne by eight mountaineers to the foot of the mountain; she was followed by two nymphs, one of whom was carrying a tricolor flag and the other the Declaration of the Rights of Man; they marched upon the trash remnants of nobility and superstition, which were then burned, to the great contentment of all the citizens, and climbing the mountain, with People's Representative Pfliéger, then present at this festival, and mountaineers who represented his colleagues, while the band played "Where can one better be than in the bosom of one's family," reached the summit. The Goddess was crowned by the graces, then a tricolor flag was displayed, and they sang "Our country's three colors," and still on the mountain they sang "When from the mountain peaks the sun," etc. The procession descended, the Goddess stopped at the spring, a vase was presented to her by the president of the Commune, she drank some water from the mountain, then presented some to the People's Representative, to all the constituted authorities, citizens and officers of the different corps present, who all drank to the health of the Republic, one and indivisible, and of the Mountain. The Goddess, again on her chair, was borne to her chariot by eight mountaineers, four others placed themselves at her sides, axes raised, to drive away the profane, the others took their places with the administrative bodies, to indicate that public dignities are consistent with virtue alone.

From there . . . they went . . . to . . . the Temple of Reason. . . .

All the musicians gathered behind the altar, with the singers; at the moment when the procession entered the Temple, the organ blared an overture, and the Société Populaire, the constituted Authorities, the surveillance committees, and the groups described above took places in rows facing the altar of Reason and a certain distance from it.

The military band played hymns to Reason, to Liberty, to hatred for tyrants, and to sacred love for the Patrie. After which the president of the Société Populaire delivered the inaugural speech, the Commune president, the Department president, the District president, the People's Representative, and General Debrun delivered speeches set forth hereafter.

After their harangues, various patriotic hymns were repeated and accompanied by the military band, after which, in front of the Temple entrance, the trumpeters announced that the inauguration festival and the ceremony were concluded.

In the evening fireworks were displayed on the mountain, a bouquet marked the gratitude of all the French to the mountaineers present, who were solemnly recognized to be the saviors of the Republic; then a ball was held, and so brotherhood was twice celebrated in a single day. Each citizen taking part in this fine day evidenced his civic spirit. All took the oath to live in freedom or to die. . . .

Proceedings of the Convention

The following excerpts from the minutes of the Convention, for February 5, 1794, exemplify reasonably well the matters that flooded before it and the procedures it ordinarily followed. The minutes were printed at the time, and have been reprinted in *Archives Parlementaires*, LXXXIV, 312, 326-329.

The *société populaire* of Pithiviers-le-Vieil, in the Loiret department, requests the Convention to continue to serve. It announces that, for the defenders of the Patrie, it is giving seventy-six shirts, three sheets, ten pairs of stockings, a towel, a pair of shoes, several pieces of linen suitable to make rags, and various objects from the former church of that place, viz.: twenty-three marks, two ounces [about eleven and a half pounds] of silver plate, a hundred pounds of brass and pewter, six pounds of tin, two bells, four canopies, and a christening-robe trimmed with fine gold and silver. . . .

A secretary read the minutes of proceedings of the morning session of 16 pluviôse.

A discussion arose on the draft of the decree adopted in that session, for the enfranchisement of the colored men in the French colonies.

Having heard several members, who agreed on the supreme justice of the principle adopted and differed only on the wording, the National Convention decreed that the Committee of Public Safety will present a final draft and the mode of execution of the principle decreed. . . .

Another member, having observed that after the National Convention has solemnly declared that the colored men in the French colonies are free, it is fitting to distribute to them the uncultivated lands on the islands and to secure for them the lands of the French émigrés, on the same conditions and with the same advantages as those in France itself. This proposal was sent to the committees on Agriculture and Public Safety. . . .

The National Convention, having heard the report of its committee on public assistance on the petition of the citizen Jean-Pierre Viennot, cobbler, resident of the commune of Pierre-Fontaine, in the Doubs department, having as dependents a wife and four young children, who after three months of detention has been acquitted by judgment of the revolutionary tribunal of Paris on the 8th of this month;

Decrees that upon presentation of the present decree, the national treasury will pay to the citizen Viennot the sum of three hundred and fifty *livres*, as public assistance, to aid him to return to his department. . . .

The National Convention, having heard the report of its committee on public assistance, on the petition of the woman citizen Braconier, resident of Libreville, in the Ardennes department, who having come to Paris to solicit release from prison for the citizen Loison, whose wife she was to become, has given birth here on the 5th of this month to a boy, for whom, as well as for herself, she asks for assistance;

Considering that for the regeneration of morals and customs, for the propagation of the virtues, and in the public interest, it is important to encourage mothers to fulfill the sacred duty of nursing and caring for their own infants; that all children without distinction belong to society, whatever the circumstances of their birth; that it is equally important to destroy the prejudices which used to cause the proscription or abandonment, at the very beginning of their existence, of those who were not born of a legitimate union; that, following these principles, the law of July 28, 1793 (old style), Title I, sec. 2, art. 4, states that "every unmarried woman who herself wants to nurse the infant she is carrying, and who needs financial assistance from the nation, will have the right to claim it," and the same law provides for institutions and assistance to be paid in kind or annual monetary assistance for all that is required in such a case by the interests of the mother and of the infant;

Decrees that, upon the presentation of the present decree, the national treasury will pay to the citizen Braconier the sum of a hundred and fifty *livres,* as temporary public assistance for herself and her infant. . . .

Robespierre's Speech on the Moral and Political Principles of Domestic Policy

The speech delivered by Robespierre in behalf of the Committee of Public Safety, in the Convention session of 17 pluviôse, is important for two reasons. It marks the high point of his struggle against divisive factions, both moderates and extremists, and it presents the outline of his vision of the Republic.

The plan of the speech is simple. After a dozen introductory paragraphs, the main proposition is stated: the Convention's policies must be guided by the principles of democratic government, and must meet the revolutionary circumstances of the war of liberty against tyranny. In the argument, which follows, each half of this proposition is developed separately. (In the version presented here, most of the omissions are from the second part of the argument.) The speech closes with a peroration on the dangers of the existing situation and the remedies for it.

Printed in pamphlet form immediately after delivery, this speech has been reprinted several times; it appears in the *Archives Parlementaires,* LXXXIV, 330-337, and Jean Poperen has edited it in a convenient selection of Robespierre's speeches.

Citizens, representatives of the people:

We set forth, some time ago, the principles of our foreign policy. We come today to develop the principles of our domestic policy.

After operating for a long time at random and as if impelled by the movement of factions opposing one another, the representatives of the French people have finally shown a character and a government. A sudden change in the Nation's fortune told Europe that there had been a regeneration among the national representatives. But, up to the very moment when I am speaking, it must be agreed, we have been guided, in such stormy circumstances, by love of the good and by awareness of our country's needs rather than by a correct theory and precise rules of conduct, which we did not even have time to sketch.

It is time to mark clearly the aim of the revolution and the end we want to reach; it is time to take account of the obstacles which still separate us from it and of the means that we ought to adopt to attain it: a simple and important idea which seems never to have been noticed. Well, how could a weak and corrupt government have dared to implement it? A king, a proud senate, a Caesar, a Cromwell, must first of all cover their plans with a religious veil, compromise with all the vices, caress all the parties, crush the party of the good men, oppress or deceive the people, to attain the aim of their perfidious ambition. If we had not had a greater task to perform, if nothing were involved but interests of a faction or of a new aristocracy, we could have believed, like certain writers even more ignorant than they are perverse, that the plan of the French revolution was plainly written in the books of Tacitus and Machiavelli, and we could have looked for the duties of the people's representatives in the history of Augustus, Tiberius, or Vespasian, or even in that of certain French legislators; for, except for a few nuances of perfidy or cruelty, all tyrants are alike.

For our part, we come today to reveal to the whole world your political secrets, in order that all the friends of our country can rally to the voice of reason and the public interest; in order that the French nation and its representatives may be respected in all the countries where the knowledge of their real principles can be obtained; in order that the intriguers who are always seeking to replace other intriguers may be judged by easy and certain rules.

Farsighted precautions are needed to make liberty's destiny depend on the truth, which is eternal, more than on men, who are ephemeral, so that if the government forgets the people's interests or if it falls back into the hands of corrupt men, in accordance with the natural course of things, the light of recognized principles will make clear its betrayals, and so that every new faction will meet death in the mere thought of crime.

Happy the people who can reach that point! For, whatever new outrages are prepared against it, what resources are presented by an order of things in which the public reason is the guarantee of liberty!

What is the end toward which we are aiming? The peaceable enjoyment of liberty and equality; the reign of that eternal justice whose laws have been graven not on marble and stone but in the hearts of all men, even the slave who forgets them and the tyrant who denies them. [Applause.] . . .

We want to substitute, in our land, morality for egotism; probity for honor; principles for customs; ethics for propriety; the rule of reason for the tyranny of fashion; disdain for vice for disdain for misfortune; self-respect for insolence; spiritual grandeur for vanity; love of glory for love of money; good men for good society; merit for intrigue; genius for wit; truth for brilliance; the charm of happiness for the boredom of sensual pleasure; human greatness for the pettiness of the great; a magnanimous, powerful, happy people for an easy, frivolous, and miserable people: that is, all the virtues and all the miracles of the republic for all the vices and all the absurdities of the monarchy. [Applause.] . . .

What is the nature of the government that can effect these prodigies? Only that government which is democratic or republican: these two words are synonyms, despite the abuses of common diction; for aristocracy is no more republican than is monarchy. Democracy is not a state in which the whole people, continually assembled, itself rules on all public business, still less is it one in which a hundred thousand fractions of the people decide, by unrelated, hasty, and contradictory measures, on the fate of the entire society; such a government has never existed, and it could exist only to lead the people back to despotism.

Democracy is a state in which the sovereign people, guided by laws which are its own work, itself does all it can do well, and through delegates all it cannot do itself.

It is, then, in the principles of democratic government that you must look for the rules of your political conduct.

But, to found and consolidate democracy, to achieve the peaceable reign of the constitutional laws, we must end the war of liberty against tyranny and pass safely across the storms of the revolution: such is the aim of the revolutionary system that you have enacted. Your conduct, then, ought also to be regulated by the stormy circumstances in which the republic is placed; and the plan of your administration must result from the spirit of the revolutionary government combined with the general principles of democracy.

Now, what is the fundamental principle of the democratic or popular government—that is, the essential spring which makes it move? It is virtue; I am speaking of the public virtue which effected so many prodigies in Greece and Rome and which ought to produce much more surprising ones in republican France; of that virtue which is nothing other than the love of country and of its laws.

But as the essence of the republic or of democracy is equality, it follows that the love of country necessarily includes the love of equality.

It is also true that this sublime sentiment assumes a preference for the public interest over every particular interest; hence the love of country presupposes or produces all the virtues: for what are they other than that spiritual strength which renders one capable of those sacrifices? And how could the slave of avarice or ambition, for example, sacrifice his idol to his country?

Not only is virtue the soul of democracy; it can exist only in that government. . . .

Only in democracy is the state really the *patrie* of all the individuals who compose it and can it count as many interested defenders of its cause as it has citizens. That is the source of the superiority of free peoples over all others. If Athens and Sparta triumphed over the tyrants of Asia, and the Swiss over the tyrants of Spain and Austria, we need not look for any other cause.

But the French are the first people of the world who have established real democracy, by calling all men to equality and to the full rights of the citizen; and there, in my opinion, is the real reason why all the tyrants in league against the Republic will be vanquished.

There are great consequences to be drawn immediately from the principles that we have just set forth.

Since the soul of the Republic is virtue, equality, and since your aim is to found, to consolidate the Republic, it follows that the first rule of your political conduct must be to relate all your operations to the maintenance of equality and the development of virtue; for the first care of the legislator ought to be to fortify the principle of the government. Thus all that tends to stir the love of country, to purify morals and customs, to elevate souls, to direct the passions of the human heart toward the public interest, ought to be adopted or established by you. All that tends to concentrate them in the abjection of the personal self, to reawaken the infatuation for petty things and disdain for great things, ought to be rejected or suppressed. In the system of the French revolution, what is immoral is impolitic, what is corruptive is counterrevolutionary. Weakness, vice, prejudice are the road to royalty. Drawn along too often, perhaps, by the weight of our old usages, as well as by the imperceptible tendency of human weakness, toward false ideas and pusillanimous feelings, we have to guard against excessive energy much less than against excessive weakness. Perhaps the greatest peril we have to avoid is not being fervent from zeal, but rather becoming tired of the good and intimidated by our own courage. So, turn ever tighter the spring of republican government, instead of letting it run down. I have no need to say here that I do not want to justify any excess. The most sacred principles are abused; it is for the government's wisdom to consider circumstances, to seize the right moment, to choose the method; to prepare great things is an essential part of doing them, as wisdom itself is part of virtue.

We do not claim to cast the French republic in the Spartan mold; we want neither the austerity nor the corruption of a cloister. What we have just presented to you, in all its purity, is the moral and political principle of popular government. You have a compass by which you can steer into the middle of the storms of passion, into the eye of the hurricane of intrigues around you. You have the touchstone by which you can test all laws, all proposals, suggested to you. By ceaselessly comparing them with that principle, you can henceforward avoid the usual peril of great assemblies, the danger of being surprised and of hasty, incoherent, and contradictory measures. You can give all your operations the cohesion, unity, wisdom, and dignity that ought to distinguish the representatives of the first people of the world.

It is not the obvious consequences of the principle of democracy that need to be presented in detail; it is rather the simple and fertile principle itself that deserves to be expounded.

Republican virtue can be considered in relation to the people and in relation to the government; it is necessary in both. When only the government lacks virtue, there remains a resource in the people's virtue; but when the people itself is corrupted, liberty is already lost.

Fortunately virtue is natural to the people, notwithstanding aristocratic prejudices. A nation is truly corrupted when, having by degrees lost its character and its liberty, it passes from democracy to aristocracy or to monarchy; that is the decrepitude and death of the body politic. . . .

But when, by prodigious efforts of courage and reason, a people breaks the chains of despotism to make them into trophies of liberty; when by the force of its moral temperament it comes, as it were, out of the arms of the death, to recapture all the vigor of youth; when by turns it is sensitive and proud, intrepid and docile, and can be stopped neither by impregnable ramparts nor by the innumerable armies of the tyrants armed against it, but stops of itself upon confronting the law's image; then if it does not climb rapidly to the summit of its destinies, this can only be the fault of those who govern it.

Besides, in a sense, one can say that to love justice and equality, the people does not need great virtue; it has only to love itself.

But the magistrate is obliged to sacrifice his interest to the people's interest, and his pride, derived from power, to equality. The law must speak imperiously above all to him who is its voice. The government must weigh heavily on all its parts, to hold them in harmony. If there exists a representative body, a primary authority constituted by the people, it must exercise ceaseless surveillance and control over all the public functionaries. But what will control it, if not its own virtue? The higher the source of public order is placed, the purer it ought to be; the representative body, then, must begin in its own midst by subduing all private passions to the general passion for the public weal. Fortunate are the representatives, when their glory and their interest itself, as much as their duties, attach them to the cause of liberty!

From all this let us deduce a great truth: the characteristic of popular government is confidence in the people and severity towards itself.

The whole development of our theory would end here if you had only to pilot the vessel of the Republic through calm waters; but the tempest roars, and the revolution imposes on you another task.

This great purity of the French revolution's basis, the very sublimity of its objective, is precisely what causes both our strength and our weakness. Our strength, because it gives to us truth's ascendancy over imposture, and the rights of the public interest over private interests; our weakness, because it rallies all vicious men against us, all those who in their hearts contemplated despoiling the people and all those who intend to let it be despoiled with impunity, both those who have rejected freedom as a personal calamity and those who have embraced the revolution as a career and the Republic as prey. Hence the defection of so many ambitious or greedy men who since the point of departure have abandoned us along the way because they did not begin the journey with the same destination in view. The two opposing spirits that have been represented in a struggle to rule nature might be said to be fighting in this great period of human history to fix irrevocably the world's destinies, and France is the scene of this fearful combat. Without, all the tyrants encircle you; within, all tyranny's friends conspire; they will conspire until hope is wrested from crime. We must smother the internal and external enemies of the Republic or perish with it; now in this situation, the first maxim of your policy ought to be to lead the people by reason and the people's enemies by terror.

If the spring of popular government in time of peace is virtue, the springs of popular government in revolution are at once *virtue and terror:* virtue, without which terror is fatal; terror, without which virtue is powerless. Terror is nothing other than justice, prompt, severe, inflexible; it is therefore an emanation of virtue; it is not so much a special principle as it is a consequence of the general principle of democracy applied to our country's most urgent needs.

It has been said that terror is the principle of despotic government. Does your government therefore resemble despotism? Yes, as the sword that gleams in the hands of the heroes of liberty resembles that with which the henchmen of tyranny are armed. Let the despot govern by terror his brutalized subjects; he is right, as a despot. Subdue by terror the enemies of liberty, and you will be right, as founders of the Republic. The government of the revolution is liberty's despotism against tyranny. Is force made only to protect crime? And is the thunderbolt not destined to strike the heads of the proud?

Nature imposes on every physical and moral being the law of striving for its own preservation: to reign, crime slaughters innocence; and in crime's hands, innocence resists with all its might. . . .

And yet one or the other must succumb. Indulgence for the royalists, cry certain men, mercy for the villains! No! mercy for the innocent, mercy for the weak, mercy for the unfortunate, mercy for humanity.

Society owes protection only to peaceable citizens; the only citizens in the Republic are the republicans. For it, the royalists, the conspirators are only strangers or, rather, enemies. This terrible war waged by liberty against tyranny—is it not indivisible? Are the enemies within not the allies of the enemies without? The assassins who tear our country apart, the intriguers who buy the consciences that hold the people's mandate; the traitors who sell them; the mercenary pamphleteers hired to dishonor the people's cause, to kill public virtue, to stir up the fire of civil discord, and to prepare political counterrevolution by moral counterrevolution—are all those men less guilty or less dangerous than the tyrants whom they serve? All who interpose their treasonous gentleness between those villains and the avenging sword of national justice resemble those who would throw themselves between the tyrants' henchmen and our soldiers' bayonets; all the impulses of their false sensitivity appear to me only sighs of longing for England and Austria. . . .

With what good humor are we still duped by words! How aristocracy and moderatism still govern us through the murderous maxims they gave us!

Aristocracy defends itself better by intrigue than patriotism does by service. We try to control revolutions with the quibbles of the courtroom; we treat conspiracies against the Republic like lawsuits between individuals. Tyranny kills, and liberty argues; and the code made by the conspirators themselves is the law by which we judge them.

Though it involves our country's safety, general report cannot be substituted for the evidence of testimony, nor obviousness itself for literal proof.

Justice delayed means immunity from punishment; possible impunity encourages all the guilty; and yet there are complaints against the severity of justice; there are complaints against the imprisonment of enemies of the Republic. Examples are sought in the histories of tyrants, because those who complain do not want to choose them in the histories of peoples, nor derive them from the natural tendency of liberty threatened. . . .

It is clemency to mankind to punish its oppressors; it is barbarism to pardon them. Tyrants' rigor has no principle but rigor; the republican government's rigor begins in charity. . . .

What frivolity it would be to regard a few victories won by patriotism as the end of all our dangers. Glance at our real situation. You will be aware that you need vigilance and energy more than ever. Sullen ill-will everywhere acts contrary to the government's operations. The fatal influence of the foreign courts, while it is more effectively hidden, is thereby neither less active nor less deadly. Crime, intimidated, has done nothing but cover its operations more adroitly.

The internal enemies of the French people are divided into two factions, like two army corps. They march under banners of different colors and by separate routes; but they are marching to the same destination: their purpose is the disorganization of popular government, the ruin of the Convention—that is, the triumph of tyranny. One of these two factions urges us to commit excesses; the other, to be weak. One wants to change liberty into drunken frenzy; the other, into prostitution. . . .

One faction has been called the moderates; the other has been designated—more cleverly perhaps than precisely—as the ultra-revolutionaries. This denomination can in no case be applied to the men of good faith who may be carried away by zeal and ignorance to actions beyond the sound policy of the revolution, and it does not characterize accurately the perfidious men whom tyranny hires to practice false and deadly applications that compromise the sacred principles of our revolution.

The false revolutionary is deficient more often than excessive in [his response to] the revolution. He is moderate or insanely patriotic, according to the circumstances. What he will think tomorrow is decided for him today by committees of Prussians, English, Austrians, even Muscovites. He opposes energetic measures and exaggerates them when he has been unable to block them. He is severe toward innocence but indulgent toward crime, accusing even the guilty who are not rich enough to purchase his silence nor important enough to merit his zeal, but carefully refraining from ever compromising himself to the point of defending virtue that has been slandered; now and then discovering plots that have already been discovered, ripping the masks off traitors who are already unmasked and even decapitated but extolling traitors who are living and still influential; always eager to embrace the opinion of the moment and as alert never to enlighten it, and above all never to clash with it; always ready to adopt bold measures provided they have many drawbacks; falsely attacking the measures that have only advantages or adding all the amendments that can render them harmful; speaking the truth sparingly but as much as he must in order to acquire the right to lie with impunity; giving forth driblets of good and torrents of evil; full of fire for great resolutions which signify nothing; worse than indifferent to those which can honor the people's cause and save our country; giving much attention to the forms of patriotism; very much attached, like the devout whose enemy he declares himself to be, to formal observances, he would prefer to wear out a hundred red caps than to accomplish one good deed. [Applause.] . . .

Do you want to put [such men] to the test? Ask them, not for oaths and declamations, but for real services.

Is action needed? They orate. Is deliberation required? They want to begin with action. Are the times peaceful? They will oppose every useful change. Are the times stormy? They will speak of reforming everything, in order to throw everything into confusion. Do you want to keep sedition in check? They remind you of Caesar's clemency. Do you want to deliver patriots from persecution? They propose to you as a model the firmness of Brutus. They discover that so-and-so was a noble when he is serving the Republic; they no longer remember this as soon as he betrays it. Is peace advantageous? They display the rewards of victory. Is war necessary? They praise the delights of peace. Must our territory be defended? They want to go and punish the tyrants beyond the mountains and seas. Must our forts be recaptured? They want to take the churches by assault and scale heaven itself. [Applause.] They forget the Austrians in order to make war on the devout. Do we need the support of faithful allies? They will declaim against all the governments in the world and propose that you put on trial the great Mogul himself. [Applause.] Do the people go to the Capitol to give thanks to the gods for their victories? They intone lugubrious chants over our previous reverses. Is it a matter of winning new victories? In our midst they sow hatreds, divisions, persecutions, and discouragement. Must we make the sovereignty of the people a reality and concentrate its strength by a strong, respected government? They discover that the principles of government injure popular sovereignty. Must we call for the rights of the people oppressed by the government? They talk only of respect for the laws and of obedience owed to the constituted authorities.

They have found an admirable expedient for promoting the efforts of the republican government: it is to disorganize it, to degrade it completely, to make war on the patriots who have contributed to our successes. . . .

Thus, for example, after having disseminated everywhere the germs of civil war by a violent attack on religious prejudices, they will seek to fortify fanaticism and aristocracy by the very measures, in favor of freedom of religious observances, that sound policy has prescribed to you. If you had left free play to the conspiracy, it would have produced, sooner or later, a terrible and universal reaction; but if you stop it, they will still seek to turn this to their account by urging that you protect the priests and the moderates. You must not even be surprised if the authors of this strategy are the very priests who most boldly confess their charlatanism.

If the patriots, carried away by a pure but thoughtless zeal, have somewhere been made the dupes of their intrigues, they will throw all the blame upon the patriots; because the principal point of their Machiavellian doctrine is to ruin the Republic by ruining the republicans, as one conquers a country by overthrowing the army which defends it. One can thereby appreciate one of their favorite principles, which is: men must count as nothing—a maxim of royal origin, which means that all the friends of liberty must be abandoned to them.

It is to be noticed that the men who seek only the public good are to be the victims of those who seek to advance themselves, and this comes from two causes: first, that the intriguers attack using the vices of the old regime; second, that the patriots defend themselves only with the virtues of the new.

Such an internal situation ought to appear worthy of all your attention, above all if you reflect that at the same time you have the tyrants of Europe to combat, 1,200,000 men under arms to maintain; and that the government is constantly obliged to repair, with energy and vigilance, all the evils which the innumerable multitude of our enemies has prepared for us during the course of five years.

What is the remedy for all these evils? We know no other than the extension of that mainspring of the Republic: virtue.

Democracy perishes by two kinds of excess: the aristocracy of those who govern or the people's scorn for the authorities whom the people itself has established, scorn which makes each clique, each individual take over the public power and lead the people, through excessive disorders, to its destruction or to the power of one man.

The double effort of the moderates and the false revolutionaries is to drive us back and forth perpetually between these two perils.

But the people's representatives can avoid them both, because government is always able to be just and wise; and, when it has that character, it is sure of the confidence of the people. . . .

It is a truth which ought to be regarded as commonplace in politics that a great body invested with the confidence of a great people can be lost only through its own failings. Your enemies know this; therefore you can be sure that they are applying themselves above all to reawaken in your midst all the passions which can further their sinister designs.

What can they do against the national representation if they do not succeed in beguiling it into impolitic acts which can supply pretexts for their criminal declamations? They are therefore necessarily obliged to obtain two kinds of agents, those who will seek to degrade it by their speeches and those, in its very midst, who will do their utmost to deceive it in order to compromise its glory and the interests of the Republic. . . .

Far from us is the idea that there still exists in our midst a single man weakling enough to intend to serve the tyrants' cause! But farther from us still is the crime, for which we would not be pardoned, of deceiving the National Convention and betraying the French people by a culpable silence! For it is the good fortune of a free people that truth, which is the scourge of despots, is always its strength and salvation. Now it is true that there still exists a danger for our liberty, perhaps the only serious danger which remains for it to confront. That danger is a plan which has existed for rallying all the enemies of the Republic by reviving party spirit; for persecuting the patriots, defeating and disheartening the faithful agents of the republican government, rendering inadequate the most essential parts of the public service. They have intended to deceive the Convention about men and about conditions; they have sought to put it on the wrong track about the causes of abuses, which they have exaggerated so as to make them irremediable; they have studiously filled it with false terrors, in order to lead it astray or paralyze it; they seek to divide it, above all to create division between the representatives sent out to the departments and the Committee of Public Safety. They have sought to influence those representatives to contradict the measures of the central authority, in order to produce disorder and confusion; they have sought to embitter them after their return, in order to make them the unknowing instruments of a cabal. The foreigners turn to their profit all private passions, even abused patriotism.

They first adopted the plan of going straight to their goal, by slandering the Committee of Public Safety; they flattered themselves aloud that it would succumb under the weight of its laborious duties. Victory and the good fortune of the French people defended it. Since that time they have adopted the plan of praising it while paralyzing it and destroying the results of its work. All those vague declamations against necessary agents of the Committee; all the proposals for disorganization, disguised under the name of reforms, already rejected by the Convention and reproduced today with a strange artificiality; that eagerness to extol the intriguers whom the Committee of Public Safety was obliged to remove; that terror inspired in good citizens; that indulgence with which conspirators are favored: that whole system of imposture and intrigue, whose principal author is a man whom you have driven from your midst, is directed against the National Convention and tends to give effect to the resolutions of all the enemies of France.

It is since the time when this system was put forward in pamphlets and given effect in public acts that aristocracy and royalism have again begun to raise their insolent heads, that patriotism has again been persecuted in a part of the Republic, that the national authority has encountered a resistance which the intriguers had begun to abandon. If these indirect attacks had served only to divide the attention and energy of those who have to carry the immense burden that you have assigned them and to distract them too often from the great measures for the public salvation in order to occupy themselves with thwarting dangerous intrigues; even so, they could be considered as a diversion useful to our enemies.

But let us be reassured, it is here that the truth has its sanctuary; it is here that the founders of the Republic reside, the avengers of humanity, and the destroyers of tyrants. [Applause.]

Here, to destroy an abuse it suffices to point it out. It suffices for us to appeal, in the name of our country, from counsels of self-love or from the weaknesses of individuals, to the virtue and the glory of the National Convention.

We call for a solemn debate upon all the subjects of its anxiety and upon everything that can influence the progress of the revolution. We adjure it not to permit any hidden particular interest to usurp ascendancy here over the general will of the assembly and the indestructible power of reason.

We will limit ourselves today to proposing that by your formal approval you sanction the moral and political truths upon which your internal administration and the stability of the Republic ought to be founded, as you have already sanctioned the principles of your conduct toward foreign peoples. Thereby you will rally all good citizens, you will take hope away from the conspirators, you will assure your progress and confound the kings' intrigues and slanders, you will honor your cause and your character in the eyes of all peoples.

Give the French people this new gage of your zeal to protect patriotism, of your inflexible justice for the guilty, and of your devotion to the people's cause. Order that the moral and political principles which we have just expounded will be proclaimed, in your name, within and without the Republic. [Applause.]

Reports of Observers for the Minister of the Interior

After the fall of the monarchy, the ministries continued to exist, increasingly dominated by the Committee of Public Safety but performing important governmental tasks. In May, 1793, the Minister of the Interior, Garat, established a system for gathering information about public opinion and circumstances or conspiracies that might affect it. He commissioned special "observers" to report to one of his subordinates. His successor (from August, 1793), Paré, continued to employ them. In the winter of 1794, a dozen reports a day were coming in from the observers in Paris and were condensed into a daily summary sent from the Ministry to the Committee of Public Safety.

The individual reports of four observers, all dated 18 pluviôse (February 6, 1794), are presented here. The antecedents of these men were various, but all were regarded in the Ministry as among the best on the staff of observers in Paris. Béraud was from La Rochelle, had taken part in revolutionary activity in the streets of Paris in the summer of 1789, had then been in Haiti and La Rochelle, and after returning to Paris in 1792 had become secretary of the Temple section assembly. Charmont was from Senlis; little else is known about him. Latour-Lamontagne had served in the army; he was from Bordeaux, where he had been active in revolutionary politics before coming to Paris in 1792. Prévost was from a village in the Paris region, had been a clerk, with the rank of corporal, in the supply service of the French Guards, later a banker's clerk, and then an employee of the Liquidation directory, where his task was putting numbers on the new paper currency (the *assignats*).

The neighborhood of the Palais-Royal (whose revolutionary name was Palais-Égalité), with its gardens and cafés, was an obvious area in which to take soundings of public opinion. Both the cafés referred to below in Béraud's report, as well as the headquarters of the Montagne section mentioned by Latour-Lamontagne, were located there. Nearby were the Tuileries palace, where the Convention sat, and adjacent gardens (known as the Jardin de la Révolution or the Jardin National). In the Place de la Révolution (renamed, in 1795, Place de la Concorde) the guillotine stood.

The number of persons executed each week was not as great

in the winter of 1794 as it was to become in the spring and summer. During the five months preceding February 6, 31 women and 238 men had been guillotined; most notable among them were Marie-Antoinette; the former Duke of Orléans; Brissot and a score of other deputies; Madame Roland; ex-mayor Bailly; and General Houchard (Custine having been executed previously). In the same period, the revolutionary tribunal had acquitted 190 persons. There were 5,434 individuals in the 25 prisons in Paris on February 5.

That evening, a political club that regularly met in the former episcopal palace hall (the Évêché), from which the club took its name, held an open meeting for all *sans-culottes*. Rumor, reported that night by Latour-Lamontagne, had it that the purpose of the meeting was to call on the Convention to expel Camille Desmoulins, a noted "indulgent," and nine other deputies. Two days later, another observer learned that the meeting voiced support for the revolutionary committees of the sections against critics who said those committees unjustly ordered too many persons to be imprisoned.)

The following reports were published in *Paris pendant la Terreur. Rapports des agents secrets du Ministre de l'Intérieur,* Pierre Caron, ed. (1910-1964), III, 349-361.

No revolution was ever so terrible as ours, they were saying in a group in the Café Corazza. If no one but the guilty fell under the law's blade, and only those with evil intentions were consigned to prison, [the revolution] would be mild; but the acts of severity that are employed every moment make it sometimes so harsh that one cannot help grumbling. Who is to blame? Those who, neglecting to attend their section [assemblies]. have let control be taken by schemers who, having had scarcely enough to live on before their rise, are now displaying a patriotism which is nearer to tyranny than to the virtues they ought to profess. If there is reason to complain of the revolutionary committees, then what is to be said of the Committee of General Security, which seems to close its eyes to their barbarity? "Do you believe," said an old man, "that if this committee was repressing their audacity there would be so many unjust imprisonments? No, you would see three thousand, four thousand, five thousand fathers restored to their children— for I am not blinded by the small number they give us in the newspapers—and the Republic, which seems to be covered with mourning cloth, would become the sanctuary of happiness."

More hindrances, more atrocities, they were saying in the Café de la République. Who would believe that certain sections are no longer willing to give certificates of civic conduct, even to those having only 1,200 *livres* of income from property and several children, to men who ask for them in order to obtain [government] positions? If this continues, they will actually destroy, abolish, and reform everything, everything will be jumbled and confused, we shall fall into chaos, and it will be every man for himself. "Don't you see," an individual answered, "that Madame Aristocracy, whom you observe in a red bonnet in your assemblies, who stamps, shouts, and calls you a villain if you are rich or if you talk sense, wants to create a scarcity of [government] positions, by a new kind of cornering the market, in order to exclude educated men from them? This plan was prepared long ago, and you have only to betake yourself to the administration that is in the Hôtel Massiac, into the offices for the sale of émigrés property by city hall, etc.; you will see many of Aristocracy's creatures who barely know how to scrawl their names. So judge for yourself how everything will go if she is allowed to take too much control."

Béraud

We have been without meat today in half of Paris. Vegetables are at insanely high prices. Many women were grumbling loudly. "Is this going to last much longer?" they were saying. "The only other thing needed to finish us would be to have the second conscription class leave [men 26 to 35 years old]: then we'd die of hunger. At least, if everything was not so expensive, there are many things we could buy; but we can't get near any of them, and that is really hard to take." Three of the most necessary commodities can be gotten only with coupons; to get these coupons one has to go to one's section, and this also causes the loss of considerable time, and that makes the merchandise still more costly. I am assured that in the Faubourg Saint-Marceau there is misery to such a point as to cause commiseration on the part of the commissioners in charge of seeing that the unfortunate have what they need, and their needs make a long list, for three-fourths of them lack everything.

The citizens are reassured by the resolution adopted by the Jacobin society [against] the departure of the second conscription class, for since about a month ago ill will had rumored it everywhere, even in the departments, to the point that in the Yonne department families were desolate: "Now," they were saying, "yesterday

the first, today the second, tomorrow the third, and then the mass."
These statements were still being made yesterday in several cafés.
But today it is different: everyone is quite content; there is hope of
conquering our enemies, since the first [conscription class, men 18
to 25 years old] has not yet been used and is still complete. This
was the tenor in the groups.

On the other hand, people are quite surprised that General
Jourdan has been replaced by Pichegru, since a great many of the
sans-culottes were counting on Jourdan to deliver the Nord [de-
partment] from the villains who are still there. "But at least," they
tell us, "our hopes are not disappointed. We have the victor of the
Rhine." They hope that he will not do as Custine and Houchard
did, that he will not say he does not know the map as those two
villains said they did not know that region.

Robespierre's report to the Convention has greatly pleased the
public; he can be assured that this speech has earned him the
public esteem, he is being so extolled to the skies. There is, I think,
no one in Paris now who does not praise him; everyone feels grateful for his spirit and ability and his love for our country.

It is again being asked that the Convention decree that coins with
the royal face will no longer be currency after some fixed date. Another citizen was saying that the citizens should be forced to take
their gold and silver coins to the mint and exchange them for
assignats, and that punishment should be inflicted on the person of
any violator. In this way we should soon end the discomfiture of
seeing before our eyes that assassin of the people who ended on the
scaffold.

Rumors are being spread that the Rhine army is retreating,
abandoning Worms, falling back on Landau, and that the generals
are doing what they can to remove from the Palatinate all the
provisions and forage and everything they can haul. "That needs
confirmation," another citizen said. "It is true that they are sending
into France everything they can, but it is not at all true that the
army has been obliged to retreat."

Tonight, at several barriers, they have arrested citizens bringing
bread, cloth, and oil, which were for the sole use of the inhabitants
in the environs of Paris.

Charmont .·.

Some vague rumors seem to be causing fear that the public peace may be troubled. There is talk of nocturnal gatherings in several places, of a plan to petition the National Convention for the expulsion of several deputies. Some persons claim that there will be a severe shake-up over this matter. But as yet there is no definite information about this; it is some posters aimed against certain deputies and the assembly held in the [former] episcopal hall that have given rise to most of the rumors which are going around and which malevolence is pleased to exaggerate. The people are very peaceable, and their confidence in their representatives keeps them from feeling any anxiety.

There have been complaints for a long time about an abuse which today apparently the police are noticing. Women begging, in order to have more effect on the sensibility of the passers-by and obtain more alms, were walking in the streets with three or four infants slung from their necks, most of whom did not belong to them and had been stolen from their real parents. Four of these wretches accused of this horrible offense were taken to the committee of the Montagne section this morning. The people viewed with the keenest satisfaction the concern to repress severely such disorders.

Leaving a group in the Revolution garden, I have just heard it said that within a week we shall have a 31st of May.

Latour-Lamontagne

The ex-marquise of Marbeuf and Payen, her steward, from the moment they came out of the Palais de Justice to the Place de la Révolution, showed effrontery and disdain for the citizens who were along their way, even to the point of scattering insults against all the spectators and the Republic, saying that today it was their turn but soon it would be ours. In the end they died as do all the villains of their stamp.

An individual says that Dufresne Saint-Léon, ex-Director General of Liquidation, was the intimate friend of Payen and, as a result, of the Marbeuf woman, that they saw each other very frequently, that she had turned over to him a house belonging to her located near the former customs barrier that used to be called the Chaillot gate, that this same Dufresne Saint-Léon, when he was Director

General of Liquidation, made an agreement with the ex-Duke of Nivernais to liquidate [the debt owed by the State to the duke] which amounted to 143,000 *livres*—for at that time they were not liquidating [claims] above 10,000 *livres*—and in which agreement, it was said, there would be 43,000 *livres* for Saint-Léon. This individual says he learned this in the office of Tiron, a notary, where the business manager of the ex-Duke of Nivernais was negotiating with a broker to sell him the official accounts for this liquidation. I have not been able to learn the name of this individual nor that of the broker.

A citizen at the Place de la Révolution said that it would be good if there were twelve revolutionary tribunals to judge the conspirators who fill the prisons in the capital and who are eating our food, and that in the prisons there are many innocent people who, by this procedure, instead of staying in prison six months would stay there only one month, and in this way would make themselves useful to the Republic like all the good citizens.

Several citizens were talking with each other about the release of Vincent and Ronsin by decree of the Convention. They were saying that it would now be proper, although they are sure of their innocence, to bring them before the revolutionary tribunal in order to have their false accusers condemned; that this procedure was followed perfectly well by the tribunal, that it should be followed for them also, and that there ought to be no exemptions from it.

Prévost .˙.

Part Six

THE INSURRECTION AGAINST THE CONVENTION, 1795

The republican government experienced a severe internal crisis in March and another in July of 1794. Each occasioned the arrest and execution of outstanding revolutionary leaders, the reorganization of essential powers of government, and important changes in general policies.

The crisis in March signified, among other things, the end of the effort by the Committee of Public Safety to maintain a balance between the two opposing groups of its critics. The leaders of each group were accused of conspiracy with a heterogeneous collection of men who had been arrested for other reasons (foreigners and royalists in the first case, crooked politicians in the second), and their discredit was sanctioned by the guillotine. First came the critics who had advocated greater severity towards counter-revolutionaries and hoarders—and if necessary a popular insurrection in Paris to purge the Convention of moderates. Most important were Hébert, assistant executive officer of the city government (the Commune) and editor of the *Père Duchesne,* a popular scurrilous newspaper; Momoro, a member of the administrative directory of the Paris department; Ronsin, commander of the paramilitary *armée révolutionnaire;* and Vincent, secretary-general of the Ministry of War. All were prominent in the Cordeliers club. They were executed March 24, with 15 co-defendants. It was then the turn of their opponents, the "indulgents," members of the Convention who had called for clemency and moderation: Danton, Delacroix, Desmoulins, and Philippeaux were executed on April 5 with four co-defendants. The execution of the Cordelier leaders caused disaffection among much of the Paris populace; the execution of Danton evoked fear and resentment in many members of the Convention. After March, the Committee of Public Safety sought to achieve patriotic unity by a new method.

In mid-April, legislation abolished the government ministries, established commissions in their stead, and centralized important powers in the Committee of Public Safety. In May, on the recommendation of Robespierre, the Convention adopted as the official religion the worship of the Supreme Being. In June, the Convention adopted the proposals of Couthon for simplifying and expediting revolutionary justice, in effect reducing the trial procedure to a verification of the identity of the prisoners and a verdict of death or acquittal. (In six weeks, from June 10 to July 27, the revolutionary tribunal in Paris acquitted 278 persons and condemned 1,376 to execution.) Each of these new developments angered, shocked, or frightened members of the Convention and particularly certain members of the Committee of General Security. The intensifying rivalry between the two governing committees was further complicated by dissension within the Committee of Public Safety, where Robespierre, Saint-Just, and Couthon became isolated from the other eight members.

The crisis at the end of July, 1794, marked the failure of the Committee of Public Safety to impose the new combination of rigor and idealism. The Convention, managed by members of the governing committees and by deputies fearful for their own safety, rebelled against the program personified by Robespierre. On and just after 9 thermidor (July 27), he, Saint-Just, and Couthon, with 115 of their political associates (the majority of whom were members of the Commune of Paris), were outlawed or arrested, captured and executed while most Paris sections once more manifested passive loyalty to the Convention.

In the last half of 1794, the revolutionary government was largely dismantled. Suspects were released from prison, the Committee of Public Safety was effectually reduced to dependence on the Convention and limited to foreign affairs, the Jacobin club of Paris and then those in other places were closed, the price ceilings were repealed, and three former members of the Committee of Public

Safety (Barère, Billaud, and Collot) were arrested. The atmosphere in the Convention increasingly resembled that of the spring of 1793 before the triumph of the Montagnards: factional strife did not disappear, but was more affected—in the absence of guiding ideas or strong leadership—by personal hatreds and rivalries. At the same time, food prices rose, during a severe bread shortage in the winter of 1795, far above tolerable levels.

The Convention Session of the 12th of Germinal

> On April 1, 1795, a large crowd entered the Convention hall just as Boissy d'Anglas was reporting on a proposal for ensuring an adequate food supply in Paris. The rest of that session is described in the following excerpt from the *Moniteur*.

Boissy was continuing his report when men, women and children, having forced the door, flooded into the Convention hall waving their hats and shouting "Bread! Bread!" The members who were sitting on the extreme left, as well as the persons who were located in the gallery above them, gave them loud applause. Some of these men had written on their hats and bonnets: "Bread and the Constitution of 1793"; others had put only the word "Bread." The great majority of the Convention at first presented a spectacle of majestic tranquillity; then it rose spontaneously, shouting "Vive la république!" The greatest agitation reigned on the extreme left. . . .

André *Dumont* replaced one of the secretaries who had occupied the chair since the beginning of the session. After great efforts, he succeeded in obtaining a little quiet. "Citizens," he said, addressing the persons in the hall, "your purpose in coming among the people's representatives was to present a request to them; but it is impossible to present it amid so great a tumult. I ask you to file out, and then meet together and name a deputation which will express your desire." (The crowd: "Bread! Bread! Bread!")

HUGUET: This movement is not an insurrection. (Some voices:

"No, no!") The citizens will respect the meeting of the people's representatives; they have for some days been more eager for the deliverance of their brothers than for bread. (A few voices: "Yes, yes! Bread, and liberty for the patriots!") For some time the patriots have been incarcerated. (A few voices: "Yes, yes!") The love of country, the necessity to re-establish the credit of the assignats, that is what brings these citizens here, and not the desire to ask for a tyrant. Do you know what people want today? The constitution of 1793. (The crowd: "Yes, yes!") I move, to calm the people, to calm our country's defenders in combat on the frontiers, to calm the wives they have left here, I move for liberty for the patriots. Give bread to the people, organize the constitution immediately. People, do not abandon your rights. (The crowd: "Yes, yes! And we ask the assembly to remain in session until we have bread.")

A man came to the rail; he asked for silence and succeeded in obtaining it. The man was Van Heck, commander of the Cité section.

"Representatives," he said, "you see before you the men of July 14, of August 10, and also of May 31. (The members on the extreme left applaud wildly.) They have sworn to live in freedom or to die, and they will maintain the constitution of 1793 and the declaration of rights. (Same applause.) It is time for the indigent class to be no longer the victim of the egotism of the rich and the greed of the merchants. (The crowd: "Yes, yes!" The members on the extreme left applaud vigorously.) Put an end to your divisions; they are tearing the country apart, and the country ought not to suffer from your hatreds. Do justice to Fréron's army, to those gentlemen with the batons. (The crowd: "Yes, yes!" Vigorous applause from the members on the extreme left.) The men who, on July 14, destroyed the Bastille were not thinking that afterwards some one would set up a thousand new ones to incarcerate the patriots. (Applause from the extreme left.) Where did all the grain go that was produced by last year's abundant harvest? (Applause on the extreme left.) Greed is at its height; people scorn the assignats, because you have enacted decrees which have made them lose confidence. (The crowd: "Yes, yes!" Applause from the extreme left.) Do not hope to restore calm and abundance without punishing the egotists. And you, sacred Mountain, who have fought for the republic, the men of July 14, of August 10, and of May 31 call upon you in this moment of crisis; you will always find them ready to sustain you, ready to shed their blood for the republic. (A few voices: "Yes, yes!")

"The citizens for whom I am speaking want the constitution of 1793; they are tired of spending nights at the bakers' doors; it is time for those who supply the food, who made the revolution, to be able to exist. We ask liberty for several thousands of fathers of patriot families, who have been incarcerated since 9 Thermidor. If you have changed the order of things which existed before this period, it is not on them that your wrath ought to fall; it is only you who are wrong. (A few voices: "Yes, yes!" Applause from the extreme left.) The Cité section is not accustomed to waste precious time, nor worthy of the fawning of Versailles. And so I have spoken to you energetically in its name." (The crowd: "Bravo!" The extreme left applauds.)

The noise in the hall interrupted the proceedings of the assembly for a long time. . . .

A citizen in the crowd asked that the people's representative who appeared to disapprove something in Van Heck's speech say so aloud.

DUHEM: Yes, let him say it! (The crowd: "Yes, yes!") . . .

THE PRESIDENT [André Dumont]: The Convention will have the courage to tell the truth. The royalists and the assassins are seeking to instigate a movement.

CHOUDIEU (pointing at the president's chair): Royalism is there!

THE PRESIDENT: They are plotting for a storm; they do not know that the lightning will fall on their heads.

RUAMPS: The lightning is your army of the Palais-Royal.

THE PRESIDENT: The Convention knows the devotion and the strength of the good citizens of Paris, and it is with the weapons of virtue that it will strike the remnants of crime.

WOMEN: "Bread! Bread!" . . .

The Thermes section appeared at the rail. Like the others, it asked the Convention not to leave its post before establishing the constitutional government.

The president replied to this section. He was again interrupted by cries of "Bread! Bread!"

CHASLES: I ask for the floor to speak against the president.

MONEL: I ask for it also.

DUHEM: President, I move that you order the good citizens who are in our midst to withdraw, to let us deliberate, in order to save the people.

THE CROWD: "Bread! Bread!" . . .

Calm was reestablished in the assembly.

The Halle-au-Blé section expressed itself approximately thus:

. . . You are obliged to remain at your post, because you have not finished your work.

The constitution was your work; today it is the law governing you, because it has become, by the sanction of the people, a national possession, because the people alone can destroy this monument on which it has set the seal of its sovereignty. Let organic laws set it promptly in motion, and let a good government make people forget the odious régime of the terror.

You have collected all the powers of government in your hands; divide them; this monstrous collection, in whatever hands it is found, is a dictatorship. Restore the activity of agriculture, the luster of commerce, the general confidence in the assignats, and the tranquillity of the French people.

When you have achieved these tasks, we shall not come with flattery to ask you to remain at your post; we shall say to you: "It is time to convoke a legislature." We shall have peace when we have a government; and even if we are still at war, this would be no reason for you to perpetuate yourselves in office, for a good constitutional government ought to serve in time of war as in time of peace.

In the name of the people, in the name of the ills that we have suffered, in the name of the widows and the orphans and all the victims of the last tyranny, in the name of the patriots assassinated, we beg you to abjure or at least to postpone your hatreds. Let a minority cease to confound license with liberty of opinion.

People talk of immediately restoring liberty to all detained persons. Yes, no doubt, prompt justice is needed; but we do not like mass discharges of prisoners any better than judgments in batches.

If you had not become administrators through your committees, you would not find it so difficult today to require accounts from those who seek to flee responsibility. A government without responsibility is not a government. (Lively applause.) . . .

Boissy d'Anglas finished his report on the food supply and the means proper to bring back abundance and contain malevolence. He revealed all the devices that have been brought into play to obstruct deliveries of supplies of food to Paris. . . .

PRIEUR, of the Marne: I move that tomorrow bread be distributed by preference to the workmen and indigent citizens and that the rice and biscuit be given to the well-to-do.

Citizens, I am going to cite a fact which will prove to you how much malevolence is acting to corrupt public opinion. An individual was making a point of displaying a piece of very fine bread; citizens surrounded him and asked him where he had gotten it. "Not everyone who wants it can have it," he replied spitefully; "it's deputy's bread." (The assembly rose in indignation.) . . .

JEANBON DE SAINT-ANDRÉ: What has happened within these walls ought to cause profound thought, and no doubt our reflections will benefit public affairs. I abstain at present from judging this event; when we are calmer, perhaps we shall find its cause, origin, and secret purpose.

Great measures are necessary to save the republic. Already you have concerned yourselves with the food supply, and you will do so again tomorrow; but this is not enough. It has been said that the assignat is below the real value it ought to have; you have heard proposed a plan for the finances; I, too, think that you ought to concern yourselves with the finances; but the discredit of the assignats ought to cause us to take larger measures. When a person offers coin, he obtains all the food he wants; thus the debasement of the currency comes not from the too great quantity of assignats but from the weakness of the government. . . .

It is important then, in order that the assignat regain its value, for food to become abundant and commerce to be revived, for the republic to be solidly based. (Applause.) Everything is interrelated in the social order, and the trunk from which all the branches grow is what needs to be invigorated, in order to make the boughs flourish. (Renewed applause.) They are right, those who told us that food supply and finances are words that it is always dangerous to utter. But the public happiness, the guarantee of property, liberty and equality, that is what we can attend to without fear. Let your committees, in the quiet of their discussions, take care of the finances and the food supply. You will ask them what they have done when you think it useful to public affairs; but while naming to the committees men worthy of your confidence, you will be careful to interrogate them as little as possible; it is for you to make the laws; it is to your committees that you ought to leave their administration.

You have often been told that you must banish hatreds from your midst; for this, several means have been proposed. I think that the one, the only, means to achieve this is to concern yourselves ceaselessly with the people's happiness. The evil by which you are affected is a contagious malady, which has spread over all France; everyone wants to govern and no one wants to obey. This is not the system indicated by wisdom; it is not the means to establish a government, to secure the republic, to dictate peace, and to restore abundance. . . .

Citizens, take another attitude. . . . To reconnect all the ties of the social system, to reestablish the value of the assignats, revive commerce, restore abundance, you must organize the republican government without delay and force everyone to believe in the republic. (Applause.)

The Convention decreed the insertion of Jeanbon's speech in the *Bulletin.*

ISABEAU: We have not been able up to now to report on all the events of the day; the Committee on General Security is still busy, with the Committee on Military Affairs and that on Public Safety, giving the orders necessitated by the circumstances. All our time has been employed in saving the public weal. Our colleague Auguis, whom the Committee on General Security had charged with going about different quarters of Paris to restore peace in them, has been attacked and wounded. . . .

This morning's gathering, like all the others, began in the Cité section, with women and children who marched to the bakers'; they prevented the peaceful citizens from receiving the portion intended for them. They obliged the constituted authorities—who, by the way, did their duty—to give them a drum which they beat in all the streets. The fire quickly kindled; people spread a thousand horrible rumors to start insurrection. They said that the Gravilliers section had been disarmed last night, that a great number of deputies had left Paris. . . . Your three committees, deeply impressed with how important it is that today's attempt against the national representation not be repeated and that the liberty of its deliberations still be preserved, has charged me to propose the following draft decree:

I. The National Convention declares to the French people that today there was an attempt against the liberty of its deliberations.

II. The Committee on General Security will investigate and will arraign before the criminal court of the department of Paris the authors and instigators of this attempt.

This draft excited violent protests on the extreme left. The members in other parts of the hall moved that it be put to a vote . . . The draft was adopted; the members of the extreme left abstained. . . .

DUMONT: Citizens, employ severity, or our country is lost. It is time to make the people know their executioners. Yes, representatives, your enemies, the people's enemies, the real royalists, are there! (Dumont pointed to the members on the extreme left. The most vigorous applause broke out everywhere; it was redoubled and prolonged.) They are not in England, but in your midst; they fill the galleries with their henchmen, and they block your good deeds. They hold secret nocturnal meetings, in which they contrive plots. I know that they have consigned me to their daggers. Well! Let all their assassins recognize me; I want to perish by their hand or save my country. (Vigorous applause.) Ought we to expect anything other than daggers from men who are strangers to probity and to all humane sentiments? (Applause.) Do you know the purpose of today's movement? It is to prevent you from deciding on the fate of three brigands who have drenched the republic with blood. (Applause.) . . .

Representatives, you complain that public opinion appears to be abandoning you. Well, if you want to keep it, be firm. (Applause.) You have proof today of the complicity and of the part that the men who are awaiting judgment [Barère, Billaud de Varennes, and Collot d'Herbois] have had in this revolt. I shall not propose that you close off debate; such a measure is fitting only for assassins. Nor shall I propose to you to sentence them to death without having had them judged; but I propose that you drive them from French territory. (Applause broke out everywhere.)

This proposal was accepted amid the most vigorous applause and at once decreed.

CRASSOUS and several other members on the extreme left asked for a roll-call; [fifty signatures being required for this] they went to the secretaries' table to sign their request.

BOURDON, of the Oise: I move that this roll-call, which is the last effort of a rebel minority, be sent to the departments. I move also for the arrest of Chasles, Choudieu, and Foussedoire. (Applause everywhere.)

The proposal was decreed. . . .

[Additional debates and accusations resulted in decrees ordering the arrest of Huguet, Bourdon (representative of the Loiret), Ruamps, and Duhem. The session ended at 6 o'clock the following morning.]

Police Commissioners' Reports

The police reporting system for the city of Paris was reorganized in April, 1794, and again at the end of July; after October, 1794, it was supervised by a 20-member police commission appointed by the Convention. There were many police inspectors (24 were assigned to surveillance of the bakers, and others to other duties). Practically no biographical details are available concerning them. The reports from the inspectors were condensed into daily summaries by two or three of the police commissioners. These summaries were sent to the administrative authorities of Paris and to the Committee of Public Safety.

Most of the summaries have been published by Alphonse Aulard. The following documents are in his collection, *Paris pendant la réaction thermidorienne et sous le Directoire* (Paris, 1898-1902), I, 627-632.

13 germinal, Year III [April 2, 1795]

Public sentiment. The events of yesterday having given rise to a series of reports, called for by the successive circumstances and dealing with publicly known facts, we have not thought it necessary to report them again; we shall limit ourselves to citing a few particular facts which have reached us and which seem to have some connection with the pretexts for the insurrection. It is reported that the workmen's discontent seemed to derive from Article 12 of the order by the Committee of Public Safety, dated 11 germinal, which provides that citizens occupying furnished houses lodging nonresidents will not take part in the distributions of food and that they are obliged to obtain supplies on the free market. In the gathering of workmen on Rue Montmartre, observers saw many stonecutters, masons, and others of the building trades, who ordinarily come to Paris at the beginning of the work season and return in the winter to their families, and during their stay here are lodged only in furnished rooms.

Dubout, inspector, reports that in the Jardin National he noticed a man, a self-styled cavalryman, making the most incendiary proposals, saying that the Convention is composed only of thieves and crooks, that it is necessary to surround them and seize the weapons supply and to appoint a twenty-four member commission to take the reins of government, that he himself would direct those who were to seize the weapons, that he was going to a printer to have something printed to enlighten the people, that this work would appear in two days, and that it would then perhaps be too late. This individual was followed to a cabaret at the corner of the Rue du Bac and the Rue de Grenelle, where he went in with a cavalryman. The drums beat general quarters at that moment, and the numerous patrols which went past in every direction caused the inspector to lose the object of his surveillance; he could no longer see him and has only his description, which we have told him to use to find him. . . .

Trade. Bread. Losset, Martin, and others indicate that the gatherings are still considerable at the bakers' doors, where there is much grumbling that the flour arrives too late at the bakers'. Various bakers provided only a quarter-loaf of bread to each individual; this small ration made the mothers of families weep, saying that they were gradually being put to death, and others made statements against the constituted authorities and the government. Despite this decrease, many persons got no bread and will not accept rice instead, in view of the shortage of wood and charcoal necessary to cook it. Several bakers are complaining that the apportionment of flour is unequal, since within the same section some are providing a pound of bread for each citizen and others half a pound. Losset observes that in the Théâtre-Français, Marchés, and Lombards sections, the drums were beating recall, for the citizens to go to the Convention to ask it for bread and find out whether the intention was to make the people die of hunger. In general, tempers were very hot in all these places. The transactions were carried out amid a lot of agitation, as many persons would not accept the quarter-loaf of bread that the bakers were trying to give them. . . .

Meat and other food. Lassiot and Drouin say that at the butchers' doors the gatherings were considerable but the meat was distributed peacefully. Losset, Loctave, and Oury report that the central markets and the Germain market were quite well provided. The provisions increase in price every day; the meat market was well supplied; it is being sold at 7 *livres* 10 *sous* a pound. In the Droits-de-l'Homme section, there are citizens who have not had bread for three days. . . .

Surveillance. Cité section. At nine o'clock in the morning, a troop of women and boys, who forced those whom they met to march with them to the Temple of Reason [formerly Cathedral of Notre-Dame] where they had the doors opened. An officer, trying to get a drummer to stop beating his drum, was threatened with being hanged from the nearest lamp-post; he barely had time to escape.

Fraternité. Agitation among the citizens in this section over the effort to give them only a quarter-loaf of bread, which they refused. Women took over the guards' post and made off with a drum, on which they beat. They wanted the members of the Civil Committee [of the section] to march with them.

Droits-de-l'Homme. Great crowds at the bakers' doors; the women were fighting among themselves, grabbing bread out of one another's hands; several were seriously hurt. The women citizens of the Fraternité section mingled with those of the Droits-de-l'Homme section, to get bread.

Faubourg Antoine. Two caissons, which were presumed to contain powder, were stopped and taken into the courtyard of the Quinze-Vingts [hospital]. The inhabitants of the faubourgs Jacques and Marcel joined with them to go in a mass to the Convention. Several bakers had closed their shops because citizens were refusing to accept a quarter-loaf per person.

Halle-au-Blé section. The drums beat recall about ten-thirty, to go to the Convention. On Rue Montmartre, near Rue Feydeau, a large gathering of journeymen masons; ten or twelve of them were running to the various workshops and making all whom they met go to the Convention. . . .

Two wagons, one of which was loaded with barrels containing saltpeter and powder, the other loaded with flour, were stopped going out by the Clichy gate; they were taken to the Convention hall; great excitement over this. . . .

Duchauffour, Hannocque-Guérin, Champenois, Duret.

14 germinal, Year III [April 3, 1795]

Public sentiment. Groups and cafés. Yesterday, there were many groups and gatherings in the Place du Carrousel and the National garden; malevolent persons were claiming that the Convention was admitting its guilt by not finally judging the [accused] citizens, Billaud, Collot, and Barère, that it was apparently afraid of the clarifications they would be able to give as to their accomplices.

All the good citizens, on the contrary, were applauding the measures taken by the National Convention, both with reference to these deputies and with reference to those placed under arrest by decree [Choudieu, Châles, Foussedoire, Huguet, Bourdon, Duhem, Ruamps, and Amar].

The malevolent were claiming also that the Committee of Public Safety was tricking the people as to the food supply and that it had no way to remedy the shortage.

In the Café de la Régence, and in some of those at the Palais-Égalité, conversations went the same way, and people added that the flour which the government bought had been taken by the English.

Mailly reports that in the Café de Chartres, a royalist revealed himself by saying that France is four times too big to be a Republic and that it could not get along without a king. There was an effort to arrest him, but he escaped in the crowd.

Another individual, in a group, shouted "Vivent les Jacobins! Join me, patriots!" He was arrested and taken to the Committee on General Security.

In the [Palais-] Égalité garden, the actions of the workmen were being attributed to citizens Choudieu, Duhem, Châles, and others, and the citizens were being requested to be peaceable and united.

Towards seven o'clock in the evening, about a hundred women, gathered in the Place des Victoires, were saying that the people's representatives were having a regiment of cavalry come to Paris, to prevent the sections from getting into the midst of the Convention when they had complaints and demands of some kind to be presented, but that they didn't care a f—, they were going to fight until they were killed.

Today, 14 germinal, the women were saying, in the gatherings at the bakers' doors, that Paris is going to be besieged and bombarded and that the Convention wants to make war on the people because they are talking of having it give an accounting. . . .

Hannocque-Guérin, Fauconnier, Thérouenne, Beurlier

"Insurrection of the People to Obtain Bread and Reconquer Their Rights"

After April 1, the tone and the general character of the information in the police reports continued unchanged for seven weeks. On May 19, unidentified persons distributed an incendiary pamphlet in the streets. The text of the pamphlet follows; from the *Moniteur* (in the reprinted edition, XXIV, 497-498).

The people, considering that whereas the government is causing them to die a brutal death from hunger; that whereas the promises it incessantly repeats are lying and deceptive;

Whereas, every citizen is reduced to envying the unfortunate fate of those whom starvation is daily piling up in their graves;

Whereas, the people would be guilty of an offense against themselves and the next generation if they did not quickly ensure the means of their subsistence and seize their rights;

Whereas, the government is unjust and tyrannical when it arbitrarily arrests, transfers from one cell to another and from one town to another, and massacres in the prisons, those who have the courage and the virtue to call out for bread and the common rights;

Whereas, a usurping and tyrannical government bases its criminal expectations and its strength only on the weakness, ignorance, and misery of the people;

Whereas, so atrocious a government can subsist only as long as we are so weak as to fear and obey it;

Whereas, the cavalry, which the government withdrew from our armies in order to weaken them, wanted to take the oath of fidelity not to this tyranny but to the people it had sworn to defend;

Whereas, the republicans in the departments and in the armies have their eyes fixed upon Paris, which would become answerable to them for any delay;

Whereas, for an oppressed people, as a whole and for each of its parts, insurrection is the most sacred of rights and the most unavoidable of duties, a requirement of the first necessity;

Whereas, it is for that portion of the people nearest the oppressors to recall them to their duties, because its position enables it to know best the source of the evil;

The people decide as follows:

I. Today, without further postponement, the men and women citizens of Paris will go in a body to the National Convention to demand:

1. Bread.
2. Abolition of the revolutionary government, which each faction in turn is misusing in order to ruin, starve, and subjugate the people;
3. Immediate proclamation and establishment of the democratic constitution of 1793;
4. The removal of the present government, its instantaneous replacement by other members chosen from within the National Convention, and the arrest of each of the members who make up the present governing committees, as guilty of the crime of *lèse-nation* and tyranny over the people;
5. Instant liberation of the citizens detained for having demanded bread and freely expressed their opinions;
6. Convocation of the primary assemblies on the 25th of prairial [June 13] next, for the replacement of all the authorities, who, until that time, will be required to conduct themselves and act constitutionally;
7. Convocation of the national legislative assembly, which will replace the Convention, on the 25th of messidor [July 13] next.

II. In carrying out the preceding and following articles, the respect due to the majesty of the French people will be observed with regard to the national representatives. The necessary measures will be taken to make sure that malevolent persons cannot abduct nor commit outrages upon the people's representatives, nor lead them into a false step. Consequently, the city gates will instantly be closed for this purpose.

Persons and property are placed under the people's protection.

III. Those representatives who may find themselves drawn away from their post, either in official costume or otherwise, will immediately be returned to the body of the assembly and placed under the people's protection.

IV. The people will take charge of the gates, the river, the semaphore, the warning cannon, the bells for sounding the tocsin, and the national guard's drums, in order that no use can be made of them.

Only citizens charged with the provisioning of Paris will have permission to enter or leave Paris so long as the insurrection lasts. Certificates will be issued to them by a committee consisting of one commissioner appointed by each section. This committee will be responsible for the certificates it issues.

Every outside provisioner will identify himself at the gates upon entering and leaving.

Messengers will come in, but will not go out until further order.

V. The cannoneers, the police, the infantry and cavalry who are in and around Paris are asked to fall in under the people's flags and unite with them in bonds of brotherhood to reconquer the common rights.

VI. Every government agent, every civil or military functionary, every individual who may attempt to oppose the measures indicated in the present orders will be regarded as an enemy of the people and punished as such.

All power not emanating from the people is suspended. Every agent or functionary of the government who does not immediately cease performing his functions will be considered as taking part in tyranny and punished as a tyrant.

VII. Whoever may propose marching against the people, to commit an outrage upon them in any way whatever, either as a whole or upon the person of one of them, will be regarded as an enemy of liberty and treated as such.

VIII. The men and women citizens of every section without distinction will start out from every point, in fraternal disorder, without waiting for the movement of those in neighboring sections, whom they will cause to march with them, so that the crafty and treacherous government can no longer muzzle the people in its usual way and treat them like a flock of sheep led by chiefs who are bought by it and who deceive us.

IX. The people will not subside until they have assured the means of subsistence, the happiness, the repose, and the liberty of all Frenchmen.

X. The people's rallying cry is: Bread and the Democratic Constitution of 1793.

Whoever, during the insurrection, does not have this slogan written in chalk on his hat will be regarded as a starver of the public and an enemy of liberty.

Every flag, banner, or ensign must likewise carry this rallying sign.

Every other rallying sign or emblem is absolutely forbidden and proscribed.

XI. An address to our brothers in the departments and in the armies will be prepared, to inform them of the reasons for the revolution and of its success, as well as of the measures taken to ensure the national welfare.

Note. There can be no doubt that the government will try to prevent the above measures from having their effect; but it will not be able to do so. It will not succeed in stopping the people's indignation and its own just punishment, even if it brings out the food which it is keeping locked up in the warehouses and saving for its infamous plans.

The Convention Session
of the 1st of Prairial

The momentous session of the National Convention on May 20 began at eleven o'clock in the morning, with the reading of correspondence received and reports of committees, which included the reading of the pamphlet calling for an *Insurrection of the People.* The Convention's response to this was a decree making Paris "responsible to the whole Republic" for injuries to its representatives, outlawing all "leaders of mobs" (defined as the first 20 individuals arrested at the head of any marching throng), and declaring itself in continuous session; it also adopted a proclamation. A crowd of women came in and began shouting "Bread! Bread!" From time to time the presiding member put his hat on, the ordinary signal for silence, and the Convention continued its proceedings, with interruptions.

The rest of the session was described in the *Moniteur* (in the reprinted edition, XXIV, 497-507, 510-515), from which the following brief excerpts are taken.

Shouts of "To arms! To arms!" began again in the Liberty salon; the armed force went there. The president put his hat on; the Convention remained calm. A battalion crossed the hall to go to the scene of the trouble, shouting "Vive la République!" Quickly the bayonets crossed; a fight began at the door that had been broken in; musket shots were fired; they were aimed at the Convention; all the members rose shouting "Vive la République!" . . .

At thirty-three minutes after three o'clock, a numerous crowd of women and men armed with muskets, pikes, and sabers entered the Convention; they all had, written on their hats: "Bread and the Constitution of '93," and they made the hall echo with the same words; they took places on the benches, which they forced the deputies to yield to them. . . . Twenty muskets were aimed at the president. Féraud, who saw this, tried to climb onto the speaker's platform to protect him with his body. An officer held his arm to help him climb up. One of the seditious men pulled him aside by his clothing. The officer, to force him to let go, struck him on the chest. The man, for revenge, fired a pistol shot which hit Féraud. He fell; he was carried off, overwhelmed with blows, dragged by the hair out into the corridor.

Several members of the Convention left their places and jumped over the benches; a few returned shortly afterward. The shouting continued; new detachments of armed men came charging into the hall; several of them aimed at the president. It was Boissy; he had his hat on; he was impassive in the face of insults; he remained in a calm and proud posture and did not seem to notice the danger. He asked the Convention for complete silence. Several citizens surrounded him. Some of these threatened him; one of them seized the seal which was on the desk; another made him put it back.

Meanwhile the tocsin was ringing in the Unity pavilion, the courtyard, the garden of the Palais National; every area was full of national guardsmen and artillery. The battalions, awaiting orders, saw filing into their midst armed men who were coming into the Convention without anyone knowing what they were going to do.

In the Convention itself, individuals were trying to get the floor; all the men who had come in tried to talk at once. The noise continued until five minutes before four o'clock, when a degree of silence was achieved. . . .

THE PRESIDENT: You are in the midst of the nation's representatives—

THE CROWD: Bread! Bread, you crook. What have you done with our money?—(These shouts gave way to tumult.)

A cannoneer, on the speaker's platform and surrounded by musketeers, read the plan of insurrection aloud. . . . It was interrupted at each moment by applause, drum rolls, and insults addressed to the whole Convention. . . .

DUQUESNOY observed to colleagues near him and the other men around him that the journalists' boxes were almost empty. He laughed loudly. The shouts began again and stopped the reading for half an hour; then it began again, amid a tumult which often prevented hearing anything. The multitude summoned the president several times to ring for silence. He did not respond. Rühl tried to quiet somewhat those who were around him. . . .

SEVERAL MEN: Down with the president!

It was six o'clock.

ROMME: I ask for the floor. (Noise.) For liberty and equality. (The crowd: "Yes, yes!") In the name of the people, I ask for the floor. (The crowd: "You have it.") A large number of good citizens — (The crowd: "We're all good citizens.") I ask for complete silence. (Noise.) I see in this hall none but republicans— ("Yes, yes!")

The president rang. (The crowd: "Down! Down!")

ROMME: I know you are all in the greatest need. I ask you, in the name of the sovereign people, to be completely silent and let the platform be free to those who wisk to speak. I am entirely devoted to the people's cause.

The governing committees are supposed to have taken measures for the delivery of provisions. (The crowd: "We don't want them; we need bread right now.")

A half-hour of noise.

People began to shout to the president, "Down! Down!"

Once again muskets were aimed at him. Those aiming them were held back by others. A head was brought in on the end of a pike. It was the unfortunate Féraud. The man carrying it stopped in front of the president. The multitude laughed and applauded at length.

When calm had been partly reestablished, the president sought to speak. . . .

The noise increased. The president ended by saying that soon there would be bread.

A shout: "Liberation of the patriots!" A woman with naked arms moved violently to the tribune. The men who were occupying the secretaries' desk were writing on papers, which they threw into the multiude: people grabbed them from one another to read them. They shouted "Liberation of the patriots! Down with the crooks! Arrest the deputies! Arrest them all!"

It was quarter after seven; a degree of silence was obtained.

VERNIER: Unfortunately the flour often does not arrive until nighttime. (Shouts.) Do not take the risk that the people will lack bread; in two days there will be enough to meet all your needs— ("Bread! Bread!") Listen to me— (Noise. "It's a trick. For three months they've been lulling us that way.")

A VOICE: Call the roll of the deputies, so we'll know whom we should arrest.

A man in the galleries: Let the Convention decree that the sections go into continuous session. (Scattered applause.) Search houses for provisions. ("Yes! Yes!") Arrest all émigrés. ("Yes! Yes!") Liberate all patriots. ("Yes! Yes!") Put into effect the constitution of '93. ("Yes! Yes!")

SEVERAL VOICES: Bring back the patriot deputies. (Noise.)

A MAN: We want a municipality for Paris.

ANOTHER: We demand that the deputies who outlawed us be outlawed themselves.

A THIRD: Arrest the deputies who are not at their post.

A FOURTH: Arrest the crooks and the cowards. (He repeated this from time to time for a half-hour.)

MANY VOICES: Vive la Montagne! Liberation of the patriots! Vivent les Jacobins! . . .

The crowd . . . climbed up into the upper part of the hall and let the deputies there come down. They sat on the lower benches; those who could not find seats stood between the benches and the speaker's platform.

SEVERAL VOICES: Call the roll and arrest those who are not at their post.

A MAN: Yes, and send lists of them to all forty-eight sections.

DELAHAYE: A roll-call has been demanded; I am far from being opposed to it; (noise) but it seems to me more urgent to consider means of providing subsistence for the citizens of Paris. (The crowd: "Roll-call!") Where do you want the deputies to sit? (Space was made for them.)

ROMME: I ask the president to put to an immediate vote the proposal I am making, as a representative of the people—to set all the patriots at liberty. (Loud applause.)

Vernier took the chair. It was nine o'clock.

THE PRESIDENT: Is there a quorum? (The crowd: "Yes! Yes!")

A MAN: I demand that the people keep their hats on, and that only the deputies raise their hats to signify approval or disapproval. (The crowd: "Yes! Yes!")

DUROY: I ask for the floor to present an amendment. I propose that the decree read as follows: "That all citizens who have been arrested for political opinions since 9 thermidor, and against whom there is no indictment, be set at liberty throughout the republic upon receipt of the decree." (Lively applause.)

ROMME: I move that the decree be sent instantly by special messengers.

DUROY: I have another amendment to propose. I move that weapons be restored to the citizens who were disarmed for alleged terrorism. . . .

All these proposals were adopted amid shouting and noise.

ROMME: To complete more promptly the salvation of our country, I request complete silence. I move the suspension of all proceedings begun against incarcerated patriots.

VERNIER inquired whether the deputies were of this opinion. A few hats were raised. The crowd shouted "Yes! Yes!" . . .

ROMME: After that decree, we must now concern ourselves with supplying bread to the people. (The crowd: "At last!") It is time to put an end to the scandal which has existed for some time in the food supply: there is plenty for those who have a lot of assignats, while the indigent are obliged to die of hunger. We are all pressed by need. (The crowd: "You've known that for a long time.") I propose that from this moment there be only one kind of bread for all. ("Yes! Yes!") In consequence, I move that it be forbidden for the caterers and pastry-makers to cook pastry (applause) and that there be house-inspections at once to look for flour. (Applause.) . . .

THE CROWD: Assignats at par!

GARNIER, of Saintes: The most urgent measure is to make sure that tomorrow there will be plenty of bread.

To achieve this, I move that the commissioners in the sections— (The crowd: "They're not needed; get rid of the commissioners!") I move that the commissioners in the sections go to the houses of pastry-makers, caterers, restaurant managers, and ask them, in the name of the people's welfare and in exchange for compensation for their costs, to give up the flour they may have so that the bakers can cook tonight.

ROMME: It is not enough to enact salutary decrees; it is necessary to make sure of the means of having them carried out.

I move for the convocation of the sections of Paris in continuous session. (Loud applause. The crowd: "And the municipality!")

I move in addition that the citizens resume their rights, that in each section they appoint the commissioners for food supply (the crowd: "And the municipality!") and that the civil committee or each section be renewed as the people desire. (Loud applause. Hats were raised.)

ROMME: I move that the decree just adopted not be carried out until the incarcerated patriots have been set free. (Loud applause. Hats were raised.)

DUROY read the draft of these proposals. He added: "Freedom for the deputies who have eluded the decree for their arrest adopted on 12 germinal and succeeding days.". . .

DUROY: I move that the three governing committees be required to send commissioners to report to us at once on their operations, and that we proceed immediately to a roll-call for the election of a commission of twenty members, who will replace them.

Hats were raised.

GOUJON: For a long time suspicions against the citizens of Paris have been spread in the departments; they have even been sowed among the troops who surround us. We must beware that some existing authority may already have ordered these troops into action. (The crowd shouts.) I move that the governing committees be replaced instantly. (Lively applause.)

The order of the day was asked for. Hats were raised. . . .

ALBITTE: You are human, and that is the only reason you are acting this way, I am convinced.

I move that the deliberations be given some order, . . . there is no secretary here. . . . Your decrees follow one another with incredible speed; . . . do not supply a pretext for someone to slander you.

I move that the members who have been with the armies serve as secretaries. (The crowd: "Yes! Yes!")

Thirion took a seat at the secretaries' table. . . .

A MEMBER on the extreme left: I move that to complete this day we abolish the death penalty.

THE CROWD: No, no!

A MEMBER: The proposal just made proves that it is not bloodthirsty terrorists who fill the Convention. I support the proposal, but I move an exception as to *émigrés* and counterfeiters of assignats.

Hats were raised.

A MEMBER: I move that the city gates be closed.

(The crowd: "Yes, yes!" Hats were raised.)

DUQUESNOY: I move that the Committee on General Security be discharged and a new one appointed immediately; that four of our colleagues be named to take its papers and suspend the members who presently compose it. If we do not take this measure today, they will do tomorrow what they did the night of 12 germinal. I move to give the committee the powers of a special commission.

Hats were raised to signify approval of Duquesnoy's proposal.

Duquesnoy, Prieur (of the Marne), Bourbotte, and Duroy were named to this commission. . . .

SOUBRANY: I ask my colleagues who have just been named to the Committee on General Security to meet at once and to take the measures necessary to prevent the tyrants of 12 germinal from bringing about another such day.

It was midnight. The four members left; they were met by a detachment of good citizens headed by Legendre, Auguis, Kervélégan, Chénier and Bergouin.

PRIEUR (of the Marne) asked Raffet, who commanded that force, whether he had the president's order to enter the Convention.

RAFFET: I owe no account to you.

PRIEUR: turning towards the crowd: Join me, *sans culottes,* join me! (Noise.)

The multitude was ordered to withdraw. It refused. The president commanded it in the name of the law. Shouts and resistance. The armed force advanced, bayonets fixed. Combat began. The crowd in revolt fled. Part of it returned to the charge and obtained a momentary success. Bourbotte, Peyssard, Édouard, Gaston, and several other members, who ordinarily sit on the extreme left, shouted "Victory!" from the speaker's platform and from their benches.

The sound of marching and many shouts of "Vive la Convention!" and "Down with the Jacobins!" were heard in the vestibule on the extreme right of the hall. This noise came nearer. A considerable armed force entered the hall and tried to make the multitude go out. Some ran to the door, others into the galleries; others escaped by the windows. The armed force took over all parts of the hall. The deputies who had made the proposals adopted by the multitude were surrounded; the representatives took their place again. The Convention, restored to liberty, was soon completely present and complete. "Down with the Jacobins! Down with the assassins!" shouted all the citizens who had freed the Convention; "Vive la Convention Nationale! Vive la République!". . .

Police Commissioners' Reports

The following summaries by police commissioners of inspectors' reports to them were edited by Aulard, *Paris pendant la réaction thermidorienne et sous le Directoire,* I, 733-743.

2 prairial, Year III [May 21, 1795]

Public sentiment. The events of yesterday are very well known and have left memories too painful to allow them to be described. Those which threaten us today are their sequel; they lead us to anticipate the sorriest of prospects. It appears, from the reports before us, that tempers are still very hot, and the details we have been able to collect give us reason to believe that the food shortage was the pretext, unfortunately only too plausible, used by agitators to mislead credulous citizens but that the popular movement, which was organized long ago, was instigated by the faction of the former leaders, who are now causing the people to demand not only bread but also the reestablishment of the Commune, the Constitution of 1793, the liberation of all the Montagnard deputies and of all the members of the former revolutionary committees. The inspectors observe that in nearly all the sections, yesterday evening, the proclamation of the new law against disturbances excited the greatest discontent and provoked outcries favoring sedition and a determined revolt against the Convention, notably against the representatives known for their principles of justice.

Cafés. Citizen Compère, inspector, reports that in the cafés and other public places where peaceable and decent citizens were talking about the day's events, they were troubled that a misguided populace applauds such dangerous measures and is used as an instrument for them by malevolent persons.

Theaters. They are closed.

Trade. Bread. Continuing loud complaints from the people at the bakers' doors. Hotheads poured out invective and extremely seditious statements against the constituted authorities; the women were especially impatient and seemed to be much more agitated; they stirred the men citizens up to disorder and urged them not to accept even a small part of the bread that was offered them; but these malign intentions were opposed by a number of prudent citizens. In the Gravilliers section, a man carrying under his arm a nine-pound loaf of barley bread, with an address on the wrapper, asked one of the women to read it to him, but when she saw that it was bread, she told her comrades, who robbed him of it and gave him only 4 *livres* in *assignats* for it.

Meat and other foods. At a number of butchers' shops, the public complained about the price of meat having been fixed at 20 *sous* a pound; the commissioners there were very badly handled.

The markets were fairly well provisioned and entirely peaceful; the merchants who ordinarily set themselves up under the umbrellas in the Innocents market were not there today.

Wood. At the landing, Citizen Collet was selling his wood at 130 *livres* a yard. The wagon-drivers continued to collect money from citizens and to make them pay 45 to 50 *livres* for hauling a yard of wood. The Commission is continuing to keep these individuals under the closest observation.

Surveillance. A leaflet read aloud yesterday morning in the Faubourg Antoine in various groups, and which was profusely distributed, notably in the Rue Saint-Denis, to the number of more than 500 copies, was the program for the insurrection. Its title was: "Insurrection of the People to Obtain Bread and Reconquer Their Rights."

At nine o'clock the tocsin rang in a number of sections; then the drums beat general quarters everywhere; a crowd of women betook themselves to the Convention; the sections of the Faubourg Antoine arrived there at two o'clock. They all had written on their hats: "Bread and the Constitution of 1793." That was the refrain of the women at the Convention. The purpose of these sections was to support the women.

A woman, one of those who succeeded in entering the Convention hall by force, having seized a saber from a policeman who was trying to push her out, had her hand seriously wounded.

In the afternoon, a large number of deputies were stopped by women and armed men. Some were ill treated; they were all taken to the section of the Committee of General Security.

Some citizens stopped Representative Garilhe and took him to the Committee of Public Safety.

Representative Féraud was assassinated, his head carried about on the end of a pike; about fifteen minutes before eight o'clock, the one who was carrying it was arrested, on Rue de la Loi, by the armed force of the Museum section, upon demand of Citizen Manigot, peace officer. He was taken to the guard house at city hall. His name is Jean Tinel, journeyman locksmith, Popincourt section. . . .

Pasté

Doillot

4 prairial, Year III [May 23, 1795]

Public sentiment. Today's reports, while informing us that yesterday there was no significant movement except what happened in the Place de Grève, which will be mentioned, still present the situation in Paris as both unfortunate and ominous. In fact, the high cost of merchandise and the scarcity of bread are still the pretext from which malevolence seeks advantage; it is chiefly the women who are being stirred up; they in turn, passing on all their frenzy to the men, stir them up with seditious statements and provoke the most violent excitement.

Groups. Everywhere yesterday, and especially during the evening, the groups were very large and were composed of workmen; their agitation was extreme; complaints broke out on all sides; the threats, against the merchants, the constituted authorities, and the Convention, were terrible; some were swearing to kill or be killed by the youths who are called *muscadins* and are regarded as the supporters of the national representatives.

The police inspectors report that the working class appeared very glad that Representative Féraud's assassin escaped punishment. But they observe that that act of violence made a great impact upon the minds of the true patriots, the only friends of the public welfare, and that most of them loudly expressed their opinions and said, "We are finished if we allow the laws to be disobeyed and the Convention to remain at the mercy of the fury of a crazed mob; we ought to form a human fortress around it and save it at the risk of our lives, both for the public safety and for ours and our families'."

Cafés. Citizen Compère reports that in the cafés in the Palais-Égalité, citizens were saying: "It is astonishing that a few deputies who have been designated by name are not under arrest like the others," and they added: "As long as the Convention takes only partial measures and does not entirely purge itself of the impure members it contains, it will still find its progress blocked and will not achieve its real purpose."

Theaters. Everything was perfectly quiet. At the Ambigu-Comique, the "Réveil du Peuple" was sung, loudly applauded, and the audience called for a repetition of the lines about the representatives. At the Opéra-Comique, when the announcement was made that the assassin of Representative Féraud had been taken away from the guards and carried in triumph in the Faubourg Antoine, the whole audience stood up and shouted "To arms!" saying "Victory or death to avenge the Convention." In fact, the play was not completed and everyone left.

Trade. Bread. Twenty-three inspectors report that people appear less agitated, because the bread ration was a little larger than usual. Nevertheless, complaints continue, about the inequality in the distribution of bread and about the constituted authorities, who are said to be nothing but crooks and scoundrels. They are also saying that the first two days of this month are only a prelude, because everyone is still ready to act. The people demand at least a half-pound of bread per person, a decrease in all food prices, and the old price to be fixed for the unharvested crop; they certainly hope that the Convention will take measures of this kind. The inspectors add that a number of individuals, enemies of the public peace, who are trying to mislead good citizens by treacherous advice, have been arrested and brought before the constituted authorities. Others, friends of order, are only trying to persuade their fellow citizens to be patient and to have the greatest confidence in the national representatives, who alone can restore abundance.

Constables are saying we ought to be surprised that there is not more bread, for plenty of flour is being brought in; people complain that the bakers are not equally supplied, in proportion to the number they have to feed. People also complain that food is being hoarded.

Meat and other foods. Fourteen inspectors inform us that the distribution of meat is being carried out legally; no complaint has come to our attention. Three others say that the markets were pretty well supplied and that quiet reigned in them.

Moyron and Murat inform us that the people are very pleased over the Convention's repeal of the decree that legalized trading in gold and silver.

Wood. Seven inspectors report that the delivery of wood and kindling was accomplished at various fuel yards and landings in good order; the Agence des Subsistances has requisitioned all the wood on Louviers island, as well as at the landing, for the bakers, which has occasioned some small complaints from the wood-corders; the wood merchants have said they would not have any more sent down the river; the wagon-drivers demand 45 to 50 *livres* for the transport of a yard of wood.

Surveillance. Yesterday's event, the seizing of the Tinel fellow, to wrest him away from the punishment to which he was condemned, is known, as well as its circumstances; it will not be described in detail here.

Observation of the events of this day and the preceding ones has left no time for looking for thieves. . . .

Rouchas

Beurlier

5 Prairial, Year III [May 24, 1795]

Public sentiment. Groups. According to the reports made yesterday, orally and in writing, hour by hour, the groups in all parts of Paris were very large and very tumultuous until seven o'clock in the evening; a large number of malevolents mingled in them, and still on the pretext of the scarcity of bread and the anxieties created by the illusory promises of the Convention, they were provoking the citizens to strong measures; the women, like furies, were stirring up the men and shouting: "We have to support our brothers in the Faubourg Antoine, get control of the representatives, and give no mercy to the merchants and *muscadins.*"

This scene was truly frightening; it seemed about to lead to total disorder, as well as to material destruction and loss of life; but according to today's reports it appears definite that yesterday between seven and eight o'clock in the evening, the courage of the real patriots who came flying to the relief of the Convention, to ensure respect for law and support the firmness and energy of the representatives, dissolved the storm which was threatening this great city. In fact, the preliminary decrees enacted against the factious persons of every kind, and notably those of the Faubourg Antoine, together with the firm and confident bearing of the troops of the line and the Parisian army that confronted the rebels, caused them to yield, which was effected without spilling a drop of blood.

At the moment when this happy news was being spread in all parts of Paris, gaiety was to be seen on every face; serenity and calm succeeded terror; all the citizens seemed full of satisfaction, and all with a unanimous voice made the air resound with shouts: "Vive le République! Vive la Convention! Down with the wild men forever!" The evening actually resembled a holiday; in some places the street corners were illuminated. The inspectors add that, passing in some streets, they heard citizens say: "If they give us bread, everything will be all right, and the agitators will no longer have a pretext." Some police agents report also that yesterday, in a number of places, it was being said that *assignats* had been distributed in the Faubourg Antoine to foment the rebellion. . . .

Cafés. According to the report of Citizen Compère, in the Café de La Régence and around the Palais Égalité, the majority of the citizens said they were for the Convention.

Theaters. Closed.

Trade. Bread. Inspectors inform us that the distribution of bread was carried out in all the places they watched, in complete tranquillity, with a ration of a four-pound loaf and some rice per person. Conversation turns only upon the present circumstances; everyone wants no blood to be shed and the guilty to be turned over to justice. Everywhere they are demanding lower food prices and unity of all the good citizens in order to defeat the factious plans that would be fatal to liberty.

According to Dejarrière, the public complains of malversation by the commissioners for distribution at the bakers' shops and of the harsh way they speak to their fellow citizens; he adds that there is a desire to find a means of putting down these tyrants, who seem to sneer at everyone else's trouble.

Lecordier declares he has learned that Chabot, a baker, Piques section, was searched and taken to the section headquarters with 40 pounds of bread, 370 pounds of flour, two sacks of biscuits, and one of rice; that they found in his cellar a quantity of moldy bread and that they put him in prison; he adds that the day before yesterday, in the Rue Mont Blanc, the bakers were made to give away four batches of bread, which were intended to be sold at 18 *sous* per pound, with three or four sacks of flour; they were turned over to the public, at the price fixed by the latter, on the basis of 25 *sous* for a sixteenth of a bushel, and bread at 10 *sous* per pound.

Meat and other foods. Eight inspectors report that a number of butchers in various sections were not able to satisfy all their customers; nevertheless, order was not troubled during the distribution.

Five inspectors say that the markets were pretty well supplied, that white beans were selling at 1500 to 1600 *livres* the bushel, red beans at 1400 to 1500 *livres,* and lentils at the same prices; that the people continue to complain of the high cost of all food; they say they would rather die than suffer this way. Arrival of 613 wagons of various provisions is reported.

Note: The inspectors have been advised to tell their fellow citizens that it is by being calm that they will persuade the citizens in the departments to supply them.

Wood. The delivery was made at various fuel yards and landings in good order.

Pilfer says that yesterday about eight o'clock in the evening some-one shouted "To arms!" in the Finistère section, that the women were stirring up the men to help the Faubourg Antoine but that the citizens did not want to, on the ground that the law prohibits them from having the drums beat general quarters without the orders of higher authorities.

Beurlier
Alletz

Further Readings

Narratives interpreting the whole revolutionary period are numerous. Those by Brinton, Goodwin, Hobsbawm, Mathiez, Rudé, and Sydenham differ in conception but all are valuable. The best introduction to the underlying causes of the revolution is still that of Tocqueville. Some of the topics he touched on are the subject of historians' conflicting views presented in three booklets edited, respectively, by Ralph W. Greenlaw, William F. Church, and Peter Amann. The year 1789 and the Year III are separately covered in brief narratives by Georges Lefebvre. (All the foregoing can be obtained in paperbound editions.) A standard manual for advancd study is by Lefebvre, *The French Revolution* (New York, 1962-1964, translation of the French edition of 1957). A longer period, a larger area, and a different emphasis are presented by Robert R. Palmer, *The Age of the Democratic Revolution* (Princeton, 1959-1964). There are excellent chapters in the *New Cambridge Modern History*, Vols. VIII and IX (Cambridge, 1965). It is helpful to consult the legislative enactments and other official documents translated by John Hall Stewart, *A Documentary Survey of the French Revolution* (New York, 1951). The other first hand materials available in English are meager and very uneven.

The insurrectionary movements of 1789, 1792, and 1795 were reported and commented on by American diplomatic representatives in Paris, notably: Thomas Jefferson, letter of July 19, 1789, and William Short, letter of November 3, 1789, in Jefferson's *Papers*, ed. Julian P. Boyd (Princeton, 1950-   ), XV, 285-291 and 530-537; Gouverneur Morris, letters of August 1 and 16, 1792, in his *Diary*, ed. Beatrix Cary Davenport (Boston, 1939), II, 482-484 and 491-496; and James Monroe, letters of April 14 and June 14, 1795, in his *Writings*, ed. Stanislaus M. Hamilton (New York, 1898-1903), II, 238-255 and 272-288. The best recent analysis of all these events is by George Rudé, *The Crowd in the French Revolution* (London, 1959), chapters 4, 5, 7, and 10. Factional politics is clarified by biographies: Oliver J. G. Welch, *Mirabeau* (London, 1951); Eloise Ellery, *Brissot* (Boston, 1915); James Matthew Thompson, *Leaders of the French Revolution* (London, 1929) and *Robespierre* (London, 1935); and Leo Gershoy, *Bertrand Barère* (Princeton, 1962).

Special studies related to the first, third, and fifth parts of this volume include the following:

I. Alun Davies, "The Origins of the French Peasant Revolution of

1789," *History*, XLIX (1964), 24-41; Georges Lefebvre, "Urban Society in the Orléanais in the Late Eighteenth Century," *Past and Present*, No. 19 (1961), pp. 46-75; Beatrice F. Hyslop, *A Guide to the General Cahiers* (New York, 1936) and "French Gild Opinion in 1789," *American Historical Review*, XLIX (1939), 252-271; Philip Dawson, "The Bourgeoisie de Robe in 1789," *French Historical Studies*, IV (1965), 1-21.

III. John McManners, *French Ecclesiastical Society under the Ancien Régime; a Study of Angers in the Eighteenth Century* (Manchester, 1960), especially chapter 14; Charles Tilly, "Civil Constitution and Counter-Revolution in Southern Anjou," *French Historical Studies*, I (1959), 172-199, and *The Vendée* (Cambridge, 1964), chapter 11.

V. Crane Brinton, *The Jacobins* (New York, 1930; paperbound, 1967); Robert R. Palmer, *Twelve Who Ruled* (Princeton, 1941; paperbound, 1965); Albert Soboul, *The Parisian Sans-Culottes and the French Revolution* (London, 1964, a translation of one-third of the French work of 1958, omitting the narrative chapters); Richard Cobb, "The Revolutionary Mentality in France, 1793-1794," *History*, XLII (1957), 181-196; Alfred Cobban, "The Fundamental Ideas of Robespierre," *English Historical Review*, LXIII (1948), 29-51; Georges Lefebvre, "Remarks on Robespierre," *French Historical Studies*, I (1958), 7-10.